SPEAK TO THESE BONES

SPEAK TO THESE BONES

BY
MARTIN DOWN

MONARCH
CROWBOROUGH

First published 1993
Reprinted 1994

ISBN 1 85424 199 0

British Library Cataloguing in Publication Data

A catalogue record for this book is available from the
British Library.

Biblical quotations are taken from the
New International Version

Designed and Produced in England for
MONARCH PUBLICATIONS
The Broadway, Crowborough, E. Sussex TN6 1HQ by
Nuprint Ltd, Harpenden, Herts AL5 4SE

CONTENTS

Author's Note   8
1. Speak to these bones   11
2. Power from on high   17
3. And immediately...   25
4. Repent for the kingdom of heaven is near   30
5. God has spoken   34
6. Be filled with the Spirit   39
7. Pray continually   46
8. Explore the land   51
9. Make a sanctuary for me   57
10. Heal the sick   65
11. You will be hated   70
12. Sing to the Lord a new song   75
13. A holy kiss   80
14. They went away   86
15. In season and out of season   92
16. From house to house   98
17. Different kinds of gifts   104
18. His dwellings shall be glorious   109
19. Many of his disciples turned back   114
20. Do not forbid speaking in tongues   120
21. The harvest is plentiful   125
22. We know in part   131

23. You are the body of Christ   136
24. Love one another   142
25. You cannot serve God and Mammon   147
26. Remember the poor   152
27. Come over into Macedonia   157
28. The leaders took the lead   163
29. I will bring them in   169
30. Teaching them to obey   176
    Epilogue   184

For Maureen
I thank God for the gift of marriage
and for my own wife—my helper,
my partner, and my love.

AUTHOR'S NOTE

EVERYTHING IN THIS book is true. It all happened over a period of about four years. I love the people I have written about, and I am in an ongoing pastoral relationship with them. So it is a delicate matter writing about them. There is always the danger of journalism: exploiting people for the sake of good copy. I trust that I have not broken their confidences. Wherever I have identified anyone by name I have shown them the manuscript, checked the facts, and obtained their consent.

I have taken particular care in recording matters which reveal the sinfulness of people. If the story were to be true I could not avoid this. Had I omitted the battles and the failures I would have been writing a fairytale. I have tried to be fair to those who have disagreed with me. I am conscious that I am a sinner also, in constant need of God's forgiveness.

I have endeavoured to conceal the actual identity of the villages where we live. We do not want to become a Mecca or a spectacle at which others come to gaze. A village community is its own private world. If, in writing this book, I have given away some of our secrets, it is not to draw attention to ourselves. God forbid that what I have written should glorify us, least of all me. I have written this book to give God the glory for what he has done, and to encourage others to believe that if he can do it here, he can do it anywhere.

ONE

—

SPEAK TO THESE BONES

'WILL YOU CHANGE the services?'
I was being interviewed as the prospective
new rector for St. George's. Two elderly
churchwardens and an elderly lay reader were rather
warily trying to size me up. They had asked the bishop
for 'a traditional priest' and were wondering if I would
be a threat to the status quo. On the other hand they
were acutely aware of the average age of the present
congregation, of the lack of younger people and of their
financial problems.

'It is not up to me to change the services,' I replied.
'The pattern of worship has to be agreed by the rector
and the church council together, and I can only change
anything with your consent.'

Two miles away in the neighbouring village, the
churchwardens of St. Nicholas' were also waiting to
interview me, for the two churches shared their rector
(as do so many Anglican churches in the countryside
today). After some fifteen years in rural ministry I had
learned to expect villages to be different. Here was a
different community, a different church with a different
outlook and a different spirit.

'Whatever you want to do, we will do,' they said.

This was not exactly the foolhardy commitment that it might have sounded, for I found out later that these people had definite convictions of their own and were not afraid to express them. Rather, it was an expression of a certain spiritual hunger, and a touching trust in me which at that moment I had done very little to deserve.

After four years outside the parish ministry of the Church of England I knew that God was calling me back to my first love and that I must go wherever he told me to go, to lead a local church (or two) into renewal. I was forty-eight and I had a very strong sense that time was short, not because the Lord was about to come again (though that is always a possibility) but because my own years of active service were now clearly numbered—only perhaps twenty more. And God had given me a burning desire to see renewal and revival come to ordinary, traditional churches. But were these two, St. George's and St. Nicholas', the ones to which God was sending me?

'Let's all pray about it, I said, as I left the church-wardens. 'My wife and I will pray about whether God wants us to come to you. You must pray about whether God wants you to have me. And we will only come if we *all* agree.'

With two such diverse parishes that was a tall order. Even the archdeacon was doubtful about finding a person acceptable to them both.

A few years before, while out of the parish ministry, I had been enticed to take up a pastorate in a new Community church. Growing from the seed of a tiny Pentecostal church, this new fellowship had drawn in charismatic Christians from the older, more established churches in the town—some were Anglicans, some were Methodists, some were Baptists. New people were now being converted and they all needed to be taught and discipled. I was approached about being their pastor.

A sense of loyalty to the Church of England had prevented me from accepting. I had not been brought up an Anglican; I had grown up in an interdenominational Free church in London. But I had joined the Church of England in my early twenties because I recognised it as the historic church of England. I was only too well aware of its faults and failings, in the past and in the present, but for all that I had a continuing conviction that this ancient church was still God's property and that he wanted to renew it, together with all the other historic denominations, in every one of its limbs and branches. It was my job to be part of that.

There were plenty of those in the new House churches and Christian fellowships with whom I mixed who believed that the new wine could not be contained in the old wineskins. The old denominations, they said, had become hardened; they put the traditions of men before the will of God; they did not want to change, and to look for their renewal was hopeless.

Looking around I could see much evidence for the truth of this: so many congregations and so many clergy and pastors turning a blind eye to what God was doing—content, apparently, to be curators of denominational museums. So often, it seemed to be Cranmer or Wesley who was the object of worship, rather than the Lord Jesus Christ, the Son of the living God.

By contrast, the new churches, often meeting in school halls, community centres and even cinemas, seemed to be where it was all happening: lively, exciting worship, growing congregations, signs and wonders, plenty of money. Such new churches were opening up everywhere. God was obviously with them. As on so many previous occasions in history, such as with the Methodists in the eighteenth century or the Pentecostals in the early twentieth century, God was having to open new branches because the old branches were rejecting the new life and growth.

But where did the failure lie? Surely it lay first and foremost in leadership, for where a church was given the right sort of leadership there seemed to be the possibility of renewal. There were Baptist churches in many places which were renewed and growing; there were Anglican churches, albeit a minority, which were experiencing all the blessings and excitement of new life. It was not the old denominations as such that were resistant to the new things God was doing but individuals: individual leaders, individual worshippers, individual congregations.

I certainly did not believe that the older churches had been rejected by God. Many a time in the days of old, the people of God had been unfaithful and disobedient, but God had not forsaken them. He had sent them prophets and pastors to recall them to him, and when they turned to him in their need he always heard their cry. Again and again in the history of the Church the hearts of God's people had become cold and careless. But again and again God had sent the fire of revival to rekindle the flames of faith. And at this time, it was not God's will to abandon the historic churches; God's will was to see them renewed, every one of them that was still called by his name.

God had given me his heart for the older churches. I longed to see the ancient churches and cathedrals full to overflowing with praising people, to see God himself moving in power in every place. I did not believe that the spiral of decline was inevitable. For nearly a century the churches of Britain had experienced nothing but contraction: falling membership, churches and chapels being made redundant and closing, the numbers in full-time ministry declining. But God could change all that; he had begun to do so already in many places. Jesus promised that he would build his church, not demolish it.

The prophet Ezekiel saw a vision of a valley full of dry bones, of people as dead as dead can be. He was inclined to despair of their ever coming to life; indeed, it seemed impossible that such bones could live. I knew the same feelings as I looked at so many of the ancient churches of England. But God had said, 'These bones are my people.' And his instruction to his servant the prophet was, 'Speak to these bones, prophesy over them with the word of God, and they shall live.' Flesh miraculously appeared to clothe the bones once more, and tendons to join them together. Finally, breath entered into them at the word of the Lord and the bodies stood up—a mighty army (Ezek 37.1-14).

This was God's word to me also: 'Speak to these bones.' It is God's word to all those whom he has called and chosen to be shepherds of the flock in the historic churches. Somewhere I was to lead an old church into new life.

Two days after my interviews with the church-wardens of St. George's and St. Nicholas', I rang up the archdeacon to tell him that as far as my wife and I were concerned we did feel that this was the right place for us to go, but we were committed to coming only if everyone concerned agreed.

'But they have already rung up,' replied the archdeacon, 'to say that they all want you to go.'

Only God could have done that.

This book contains the lessons I have learned in the process of leading these two churches into renewal. I hope it will encourage others to take up the challenge and the calling to do the same thing.

TWO

POWER FROM ON HIGH

No STREET LIGHTS HERE! The villagers were parking their cars in the school playground and making their way through the darkness of the December evening to the church. I was about to be licensed as priest-in-charge of the parishes of St. George's and St. Nicholas'. The parishioners were turning out for their first glimpse of the new inhabitants of the rectory. The older ones among them had seen many a parson come and go, and were not going to be easily moved, whoever he was. The committed church people were more than curious to see what this new man (and his wife) were like.

So there I stood, the object of their interest and attention—at least for the evening—and the bishop read out the words which gave me authority to minister amongst them in the name of God.

Among the visitors in the congregation were my parents, now elderly. It was they who had taken me to church in infancy to be baptised. With them I had gone to church and to Sunday school from my earliest years. It was they who had read to me the stories of the Bible. They had done all that Christian parents could do to bring me up within the family of our church and to teach me the Christian way. And in the end their labour in the Lord had not been in vain.

But in between then and now there had been years when I had gone away from the Lord, unhappy years for me and God. A significant moment had come one day at school when I was thirteen. As these moments so often do, it came upon me unawares and found me wanting: I was challenged before my schoolfriends about my attachment to Jesus and I denied it. It all seemed trivial enough at the time, but it had been a real battle in the heavenly places and, like Peter, I had denied my Lord. I was to fail even more badly a year or two later. As I watched a missionary film one evening after church I felt the Lord's calling on my life and, like Jonah, I fled from the presence of the Lord.

It is not surprising that during the years that followed my faith died. I could not face the living God, and so of course the outward forms of religion—Bible reading, prayer, going to church—slowly lost their meaning and stopped. By the time I went away to university I was describing myself as an agnostic, and my first year at college did not take me to any Christian place of worship at all.

But God had not finished with me yet. During my second year at college, he spoke to me one morning. We had a short conversation in my room: he had not appeared, but his words had been audible to me and I had been shaken to the very core. It was a week before I could continue any academic work at all and two years before I was able to say the simple yes that he required of me. But as I walked home through the wood behind our house one September evening two years later, I surrendered my life to Jesus, as my Lord and my long-suffering Saviour.

The relief, the peace and the joy were profound. I announced to my parents that evening that I was going to offer myself for ordination, and some three years later I entered the ministry of the Church of England. I knew I was called to be a missionary, that is, one sent out to preach the gospel and to win men and women for Christ. I often wondered if I was meant to go abroad, but those doors never opened while others did. God gave me a love for the English countryside and village life, and for country parishes. I became an English country parson.

As a young vicar, I was a blue-eyed boy. I was bright intellectually and nice to know socially. I worked hard in the parish. I took up the latest fashionable ideas and put them into practice. I was a good organizer and a fixer. I was told I preached 'interesting' sermons. I might at one time have been heading for high places in the Church of England, perhaps even a bishopric. But underneath the competence and the charm nothing much had actually been happening. It was not that my own spiritual life was dead: I found the Bible a pleasure to read; my own prayers were genuine, if formal—I had wrestled with God too long not to know he was real. But my ministry seemed to be almost totally ineffectual. I was keeping the show on the road, but that was all.

As a parish we did all the right things. We kept up with liturgical reform and had modern services, but still no one came to them. We had a Christian Stewardship campaign, but we still only just managed to pay the bills. We introduced house groups, and a house group would run quite happily while I was there, but if I left it would fall flat on its face. We had a parish mission, with months of preparation and a visiting team of missioners, but only one person was converted, and she attended the church anyway. I was doing my best, and it was not a bad best by most people's standards, but nothing was happening.

It was during this time, in the early 1970s, that I first heard about the charismatic movement. First there were rumours of what was happening at St. Michael le Belfry in York. Then there was a conference in Lincoln conducted by Michael Harper of the Fountain Trust; curious, I went along. Michael contrasted the life of the church today with the book of Acts. We preached to the same old faithfuls week in and week out; Peter's sermon converted 3,000 in a single day. We visited the sick; the apostles healed them. We had problems paying the church bills; the early Christians sold land and houses and laid the money at the apostles' feet. We buried the dead; the apostles raised them. I was convicted by every word.

What was the difference? Michael Harper maintained that the first Christians had received the baptism of the Holy Spirit while we had not. The power that we saw in them was the 'power from on high' (Luke 24:49, see also Acts 1:8). We did not have it. But we could have it if we asked for it.

I was puzzled and defensive. Why didn't I have this power? I had been confirmed by the bishop. Had he not prayed that I should increase in the Holy Spirit more and more? I had been ordained by the bishop. Had he not prayed down the Holy Spirit upon me for the office and work of a deacon and a priest in the Church of God? How could I lack anything? These were theological questions, but this new teaching also touched me at a deeper, more personal level. I was doing my best and in the spiritually approved manner I was offering my best in the Lord's service. It was true that my best did not seem to be advancing the kingdom of God very much, but what were the implications of what I was now being told? That it was not 'my best' that God wanted? That he wanted to do things that I could not do, like healing people or making people speak in tongues?

Then again, how could I go back to the parish and tell them that up to now I had been doing it all wrong? I was the one who was supposed to know it all. I had been to college and theological college; I was their teacher. And now there seemed to be a possibility that there was something, even something very important, that I simply did not know about. If what Michael Harper had said about the baptism of the Holy Spirit was true, why had I not heard about it before?

At that conference I caught a glimpse of something more, but the conference ended before I had comprehended what it was, or had been able to lay hold of it for myself. So I went back to the parish wistful and dissatisfied, and it was another ten years before I met anyone who talked like that again.

Then in 1983 a woman from one of our parishes (different parishes by this time) asked to come and see me by appointment. She was a faithful worshipper, an intelligent and cultivated woman and a good friend. 'I have to tell you, as my rector,' she announced, 'that I have been baptised with the Holy Spirit. Do you know what that means?'

As she told me this, something within me leaped, like John the Baptist in Elizabeth's womb. 'Congratulations,' I replied, rather lamely. 'I think I know what you mean. Tell me about it.' So she told me about how a friend of hers had talked to her about the baptism of the Holy Spirit and had finally prayed with her for it.

At the end of the conversation she stood up to go and I was not prepared for what came next. 'And what about you?'

I mumbled a bit, as I truly did not know what the answer was. 'Have you been baptised with the Holy Spirit?' she insisted. And I had to reply, 'No, I don't think I have. I don't know why not. But I don't recognise what you are talking about in my own experience.' But this time I was hooked. Not many weeks later I was listening to Bishop Richard Hare telling a Full Gospel Businessmen's dinner about how he had been through the whole process which I now recognised in myself. He too had been discomfitted by the charismatics and their talk. He too had seen that there was something there too powerful to be ignored. Eventually he had found himself asking a group of astonished Methodists to pray for him. 'What do you want?' they said.

'I don't know,' he replied, 'but whatever is going, I want it.' And he got it.

That was enough for me. Now I was ready. When the time came for prayer, it was for me too. And a friend beside me simply asked God to fill me with the Holy Spirit, which he did.

It was not a sensational experience. I was not slain by the Spirit and I did not feel light or warmth. In fact I did not feel anything. Immediately afterwards I wondered if anything had happened at all. But as the days and weeks and months followed I knew that that evening had worked a greater change in me than any since the one when I had first surrendered my life to God in 1962. It was 29th June 1983. What had I done? I had seen and heard, I had not fully understood, but I had believed and asked. God had done the rest.

The greatest change in me was simply in my expectation of God. Without ever consciously formulating the idea, I had up until then conceived of God as an elderly invalid who was confined to his room upstairs. To look after his household and his business he hired people like me. From time to time I would go up and have a chat with the old boy, and I enjoyed his company. I would take care to read the instructions which he had written down for me. Otherwise it was up to me. No wonder nothing much had ever happened.

Now I knew that the God whom I had treated as an elderly invalid was the Mighty One, the Creator of the starry height, who bared his holy arm, and whose purpose would not be denied. I now perceived that my relationship with him was not like that of Jeeves to an ailing Bertie Wooster, but as Robin to a supernatural Batman. When faced with some insoluble problem, I would now say, 'What are we going to do, Batman?' Then I would stand back and watch him do it. There might be some little task for me to do, which as like as not I would bungle, but he would manage all the same. My greatest contribution to the show would be to say 'Wow!'

So there I was, standing before the bishop as he solemnly intoned:

'David, by Divine Permission Bishop, to our well beloved in Christ, Martin John Down, Clerk, Master of Arts, Greeting. We do by these Presents appoint you, and give and grant unto you Our Licence and authority, to perform the office of Priest in charge in the Parish Churches of St. George's and St. Nicholas', in preaching the Word of God, in Ministering the Holy Sacraments, and in reading the common Prayers, and performing all other Ecclesiastical Duties belonging to the said Office.'

As we all went away after the service that night, the people to their homes in the two villages and my wife Maureen and I to our new home at the rectory, they had a new parson, and I had a new charge from God.

—

THREE

AND IMMEDIATELY...

OW DO YOU lay hands on someone standing on the other side of a shop counter? Especially when other customers may walk in at any minute. Do you lie across the counter? Or do you, like one of the Three Musketeers, leap over the counter with one powerful bound?

Maureen and I were standing in the village electrical shop, owned by John, one of our churchwardens. We were talking to his wife, Christine, who was behind the counter.

On the evening that we moved into the new rectory, the two churchwardens and their wives had invited us out to supper with them. With our own saucepans still at the bottom of some packing case this was a very thoughtful and welcome treat. So we went round to the School House, for Alan was the headmaster of the village primary school as well as a churchwarden. Over the meal we inferred from the conversation that Christine had an appointment to see a hospital consultant in the near future, and that she was in some anxiety about the outcome. As we were more or less complete strangers, we did not enquire any further at supper, but as we walked back to the rectory God was speaking very clearly to me.

'We've got to go up to the shop in the morning,' I said to Maureen, 'and find out what's the matter with Christine and offer to pray with her.'

Maureen agreed, but I still had a spiritual battle to fight that night, one of many that was to come, as I stepped out in faith and obedience to God. All the usual objections started to present themselves to me, plus a few more special to the occasion. 'But they don't know anything about the healing ministry here. Ought they not to have some teaching about it first? Suppose you pray for Christine and she is not healed. That will queer the pitch, not only for Christine, but for everyone else who hears about it. (And one of the joys of village life is that everyone hears about everything). This is too soon.'

God on the other hand was saying something different. Or at least I thought he was. Because, of course, you can't be sure. We walk by faith, not by sight. That is why faith is a four-letter word, spelt R.I.S.K. But there was definitely another voice saying to me, against all my natural inclinations: start off as you mean to go on; if you funk this one it will be twice as hard to do it next time; a demonstration of the healing ministry is more effective than any amount of mere talk about it. 'In fact,' God seemed to be saying, 'I have provided this opportunity, at the very beginning of your ministry here, to show my power. Like Lazarus, "this sickness will not end in death. No, it is for God's glory so that God's Son may be glorified through it" (John 11:4).'

So it was that the next morning I was standing in the shop wondering how to lay hands on the person behind the counter.

'What is it that you have to go to hospital for?' I asked Christine.

'I've got a very enlarged ovary,' she replied. 'It's as big as a hen's egg, and it ought to be about the size of a thumb nail. It's such a big lump that I can feel it myself in my tummy. I've been getting really worried about it, and when I went to the doctor he said I needed an appointment with a specialist as soon as possible. So I went on Tuesday and the consultant said she wanted me to have a scan, and then she would decide what to do. So I have to go back for a scan next week.'

'Well, we believe that Jesus heals today just like he did in the Bible,' I said. 'Would you like us to pray for you?'

'Oh yes please,' said Christine. There was a pause while I realized that she thought I meant that we would add her name to a list for our private prayers at home.

'No, I mean now,' I said. 'We'd like to lay hands on you and pray for you now.'

'Oh, alright,' she said, a little surprised, but quite willing. 'Where shall we go? What do I do?'

'I think you'd better come round to our side of the counter,' I said, 'and we'll just hope nobody else comes in.'

So Christine came round to our side of the counter, and stood with eyes shut and her hands open, while Maureen and I laid a hand each on her shoulders and head. 'Dear Lord Jesus,' we prayed, 'you healed all manner of sickness and all manner of disease among the people when you were on earth. We ask you to heal Christine of this lump in her tummy now, for your holy name's sake.' And everybody said 'Amen'.

'And Lord,' something made me go on, 'please make it so that when she goes to hospital the ovary is completely normal.' And everybody said 'Amen' again. Phew, no customers had come in.

As we walked back down the road Maureen and I said to God, 'We've done our bit, Lord. Now it's up to you. We trust you to do your stuff.'

For the next few days we were busy unpacking tea-chests, hanging curtains and pictures and doing all the work that follows moving house, so we did not see Christine again for a while. But we knew that she had been to the hospital and had her scan. I did not know whether I wanted to hear the result or not. I was getting the same sort of 'interference', telling me that nothing had happened, the specialist had diagnosed the worst, the disease was going to take its inexorable, dispiriting course. I just did not want to hear all that confirmed from Christine's own mouth.

It was with a faint heart that I asked Christine when I next saw her, 'How did it go?'

And it was just like it always is in the books! 'That's a wonderful thing,' Christine replied. 'I got to the hospital, and I had the scan. And the woman said, "What are you here for? There is nothing wrong with you. Your ovaries are completely normal." So I'm perfectly alright. Isn't that amazing?'

So it was. God is. No one was more amazed than Christine, except perhaps me. He had been talking to me and I had heard him. It was right to go and pray with Christine, even to pray that when she went to hospital there would be nothing wrong. He had done it. He had set up Christine, it seemed, as a special demon-stration of what I had not even had time to tell them— that God has power to heal in Jesus' name.

My faith and gratitude to him went sky-high. It was the first of many such experiences to come, and I got to know well all the feelings: God's prompting, my own fear and trembling, all the persuasive reasons for doing something else, the courage to step out in faith, and the excitement and praise of seeing God at work. Of course there would be other times too when I did it wrong, or misheard, or failed to be obedient, or when for some other reason God did not seem to act. We would all have to come to terms with that other side of taking risks for God. But for now, almost before we had begun, God had glorified his servant Jesus in a wonderful and beautiful way, and Christine, Maureen and I praised his marvellous name.

And of course, the word spread...

FOUR

REPENT FOR THE KINGDOM OF HEAVEN IS NEAR

CHRISTMAS WAS COMING, and the Church of England was observing Advent. The Scriptures prescribed for my first Sunday in these new parishes were focused on the ministry of John the Baptist. I could identify with that. It was the special work of John the Baptist to prepare the way for Jesus to come, to call the people to repentance and make them ready to receive him. The lovely old collect in the Prayer Book specifically linked this ministry of John the Baptist with the ministry today:

> O Lord Jesu Christ, who at thy first coming didst send thy messenger to prepare thy way before thee: Grant that the ministers and stewards of thy mysteries may likewise so prepare and make ready thy way, by turning the hearts of the disobedient to the wisdom of the just, that at thy second coming to judge the world, we may be found an acceptable people in thy sight.

So that must be my first job as a minister and steward of God's mysteries, in St. George's and St. Nicholas': to stand, as it were, in the place of John the Baptist, call the people to a new act of repentance and faith, and prepare the way for Jesus to come into the midst of us and do his work among us.

As I was preparing the sermons for this first Sunday I was prompted again to start off as I meant to go on. Many years before I had been told that I preached 'interesting' sermons. At the time I had taken that to be a compliment. It seemed at least to be better than preaching uninteresting sermons. But was that really the purpose of sermons, only to interest people for ten minutes? Since being baptized in the Spirit I had had a new urgency about preaching. The word of God was supposed to be living and active, not just interesting, certainly not boring. Sermons should be life-changing experiences!

If that was to be the case then the preacher had to have his eye not just on what God wanted his people to know but on what God wanted his people to do. One of my first lessons in preaching had taught me that the preacher should be able to summarise the message of his sermon in a single sentence. That sentence would often of course be a verse from the Bible, the text of the sermon. I realised that the preacher also needed to be able to define the response that that word required as well.

So what was the response that I would be calling upon the people to make? John the Baptist had called upon the people of his generation to be baptised in the river Jordan. That was not exactly appropriate for us, but I had the feeling that some sort of public act of witness or commitment would be timely. Here was I, about to start a new ministry in these churches, and here were the people, for whom this must also be some sort of a new chapter in the story of their life together. So why not let us all repent afresh, and turn to Christ afresh in faith and obedience? But what could we do to signify this? Billy Graham is always supposed to say, 'Now I want you to get up out of your seats.' But could I say that? In a Church of England service? In country parishes?

Here began again that series of protests arising in my mind, raising all the objections that seemed so valid: this is too soon; they aren't used to that sort of thing; country people do not respond quickly or openly anyway; Anglicans would never do it; nothing will happen, and I, on my first day in these new churches, will be left standing at the front with egg on my face. And all the time, I knew in my heart that that was exactly what I had to do, the risk that I had to take. I had never done this before, and I guessed that the people had never done it before either (unless some of them happened to have been to hear Billy Graham). But then, the Jews had never done it before in the days of John the Baptist, and they had responded.

I was trembling as I stood in the pulpit, preaching my first sermon at St. George's. I knew what was coming even if they did not. I preached to them about John the Baptist, about preparing to receive Jesus, about repentance and forgiveness and the washing away of sin. Then I said it.

'Now I want you to get up out of your seats. I want you to come and stand with me at the front of the church, as a sign that you repent of your sins, that you want to claim the forgiveness which Jesus offers and that you commit your life with me to his obedience. This is not a ceremony. This is for real. Don't do it unless you mean it. But if God is touching your heart to do this with me, come forward now.'

I went down from the pulpit and waited at the front

of the church. Sure enough people began to move. As some did, others began to believe their ears, and they started to do the same. Soon most of the congregation, with the exception of perhaps half a dozen people in various parts of the church, were standing round me.

I smiled at them and said 'Bless you'. Then I prayed the sinner's prayer for us all. 'Lord Jesus Christ, I confess that I am a sinner. Thank you for dying for me, to take away my sin. I accept your forgiveness. Help me to live the rest of my life in obedience to you, my Lord and Saviour. Amen.'

At St. Nicholas', an hour and a half later, the response was just as good: only two or three people remained in their seats. In a funny way I admired the courage of those who had stayed put; it is not easy in any circumstances to be the odd one out. But I also admired the courage of those forty or fifty ordinary members of the Church of England who had broken the habits of a lifetime and got up out of their seats in response to an altar-call.

In the next couple of weeks I began to learn how much some people had been moved by that experience. Someone told me, 'By the time you finished that sermon, Peter's pew was feeling like a hot stove. He could not wait to get off it.' And Sandra said, 'I had never done anything like that before, in all the years I have been going to church. And ever since, I've felt great.'

—

FIVE

GOD HAS SPOKEN

I HAD BEEN cured of white Christmases ten years before. One year the village in which we then lived was covered in a thick blanket of snow before Christmas, as pretty as a picture. But on Christmas Eve the church heating system froze solid. The temperature was so far below zero that even the heating oil was frozen. The Sunday school Nativity play commenced in a numbingly cold church, with the angels so wrapped up in woolies under their white sheets that they looked like little Michelin men with wings. The horsebox bringing the live donkey (well, it had seemed a good idea in November) stuck fast in a snow drift. The poor creature was forced to get out and walk through the snow to church just as on all the Christmas cards. But by the time he arrived at church he was in such a bad temper that instead of carrying Mary up the aisle to Bethlehem, he bit Joseph's hand. Joseph howled and had to be given first aid, and Mary made her way to the manger without either husband or donkey. Since then, if I ever dream of a white Christmas it is in nightmares.

This year Christmas was 'green', and mild. These new parishes, like most, had their own arrangements for decorating their churches, which swung into action regardless of the rector. A heap of laurel and holly branches appeared outside the porch. Ladies turned up and arranged flowers for the windowsills. A local farmer cut a Christmas tree and brought it down on a tractor and trailer. In one village the school came over to church for a carol service on the last day of term. In the other the Sunday school held a Christingle service.

And soon it was Christmas itself, with the bells ringing at night to call people to the midnight services, and the warm churches smelling of Christmas trees and candles. 'Hark, the herald angels sing, Glory to the newborn King.' 'O come, let us adore him.'

How much is mere sentimentality? How much is a real spark of faith still smouldering in the flax? So many people come to church at Christmas who do not come at any other time, not even at Easter. What mixture of motives brings them along? Who knows? And what do we say to them when they come? And are they listening anyway, at midnight, after a party in the pub or a long day cooking and wrapping up presents? Some are listening, even if a bit sceptically, sceptical of God and sceptical of the Church. Let them hear the gospel then. That at least was what I had been told and what I believed.

So I told them that Christmas about the God who has spoken, the God who speaks, a God who 'spoke to our forefathers through the prophets at many times and in various ways, but who in these last days has spoken to us by his Son' (Heb 1:1–2). If we try to find out about God for ourselves we grope, like people in the dark. We gaze up into the sky at night and shout at the stars, 'Is there anyone there?', but the stars just shine silently back at us and revolve in their courses. They twinkle, but do not speak. Then out of the silence comes a word, the word of God, spoken to Abraham, to Isaac and to Jacob, to Moses and the prophets. Finally it is the word of God speaking to us through Jesus, 'Truly, truly, I say to you ...': the Word made flesh.

And for us, it is the Bible, the record of what God has said, through the prophets and through his Son Jesus. This is how God's self-revelation comes to us: God discloses himself, his purpose for us and for our lives, his promises and his commandments, through the Bible.

When I arrived to be interviewed by the church-wardens of St. George's some months before, they had wanted some reassurance about my orthodoxy. That was not how they put it, but they wanted a parson who believed in the Virgin Birth and the empty tomb and things like that. I had been able to reassure them that I would take the Scriptures as the rule for both our belief and our practice.

That was indeed my considered and mature position. After all, what else do we have? Only my opinion or your opinion or someone else's opinion. And who are we, living so far away in time and place from the historic point of God's revelation? I am not unaware of the complexities of Scripture or of the difficulties it presents. I do not call myself a fundamentalist: I recognize discrepancies and inconsistencies in the Scriptures. But at the end of the day I believe that God has spoken to us through his ancient people the Jews, and then finally and completely through his everlasting Son Jesus Christ; I believe that God has caused that revelation to be written down, and has inspired the writing of it in the Bible.

This is a faith which has stood the test of time in my

own life. God has spoken to me through the Scriptures; the Bible daily nourishes my spiritual life. And I know and can conceive of no other foundation on which the life of the church can be built. What does it mean to be a Christian? What sort of a body does God want the church to be? In this church or that church, are we doing what the church should be doing? Too often our ideas are merely the traditions we have inherited, the common wisdom or foolishness of folklore or church-practice. We need some more objective standard than merely what our elders have said and done or the passing fashions or ideas of our own age. That standard is what God has given us in the Bible. Here we look for the truth beyond our own ideas or inherited customs. Here we find God still speaking to us about his nature and purposes for us and his church.

Leading an old church into renewal means introducing many things which seem to be new; that is the point of it. By what authority do we make such innovations? There can be only one justification: that they are not really innovations at all, but only the recovery or renewal of what was always authentic Christianity, as measured by the rule or canon of Scripture. That is what the Scriptures are there for, to tell us what the faith and practice of the apostles was. In the one catholic and apostolic church that is sufficient.

The Church of England, like most churches, states explicitly in its official formularies that its doctrine is 'grounded in the Holy Scriptures', and that the Holy Scriptures contain 'everything necessary to salvation'. What cannot be shown to be contained in Scripture cannot be required of anyone or of any church, but if something can be shown from Scripture to be part of the apostolic faith it needs no further justification. The word of God is truly the sword of the Spirit. Many a time since that first Christmas I have appreciated the importance of keeping that sword firmly in my hand.

—

SIX

BE FILLED WITH
THE SPIRIT

S USAN KNELT DOWN on the kitchen floor. Maureen
was a trifle surprised, but put down the plate of
mince pies. Susan put her hands on Maureen's
waist, while Maureen put her hands on Sue's head.
'Dear Lord, please fill Susan with the Holy Spirit as you
filled the disciples on the day of Pentecost. And please
cure Susan's cystitis, in Jesus' name.' The Bible study
group and I went on chatting in the rectory drawing-
room, oblivious of what was happening in the kitchen.
If the coffee and mince pies were longer than usual
coming in, we did not notice.

Each parish had a Bible study group which had gone
on meeting even during the interregnum. The one at St.
Nicholas' always met, I was told, at the rectory. So here
they were sitting round a big log fire burning in the
open fire place. We had, at my suggestion, spent the
evening telling each other about ourselves: 'the story of
me and God'. That way we had found out something of
the history of these assorted parishioners, and Maureen
and I had been able to introduce ourselves. We had
taken the opportunity, of course, to tell them about our
baptism in the Holy Spirit. In my experience, ten words

of testimony have always been worth a hundred words of argument.

It would not be true to say that these folk were just like the Ephesians on Paul's first visit, who had not even heard that there was a Holy Spirit. They had all been churchgoers, many of them all their lives, but the Holy Spirit was not much more than a part of a formula: 'In the name of the Father and of the Son and of the Holy Spirit.' Christine had a daughter Louise who had been baptised in the Holy Spirit while at college, and was now married in another part of the country. That was about as near as this teaching had come to them.

Maureen and I had also mentioned our experience of being healed by God. Maureen had been healed of chronic back trouble, and I had been healed, many years before, of a gastric ulcer.

Susan wanted it all. She leaped up and offered to help with the coffee as soon as Maureen went out to fetch it. In the kitchen she told Maureen how she had been suffering from cystitis. It was a recurring problem and this particular bout was proving very persistent. She had been to the doctor but the prescription did not seem to be having any effect. 'Do you think Jesus can heal it?' Susan asked.

'I am sure he can,' Maureen replied, pouring hot water on to the coffee. 'Have you been baptised in the Holy Spirit?' she added.

'No. I don't think so,' said Sue, 'but I want to be. What do I have to do?'

'We just pray for you,' said Maureen.

'Go on then,' said Sue, kneeling down on the kitchen floor.

As Maureen prayed, Susan knew that she had been

healed of cystitis. That night and the next day she began to experience the evidence. The cystitis cleared up completely and has never returned since. Like Maureen and me, Sue's experience of being baptised in the Spirit was not sensational (apart from the healing). But that night started a new spiritual growth and many changes in Sue's life which have gone on ever since and have been visible to us all. Sue was our first!

Soon after Christmas there comes a Sunday when the Church of England prescribes that we read the story of the baptism of Jesus. As I prayed about that Sunday's sermon I knew that I had to pick up with John the Baptist where I had left off a few weeks before. 'I baptise you with water,' John had said, 'but the one who comes after me will baptise you with the Holy Spirit' (Luke 3:16). Now I must preach the baptism of the Holy Spirit, and I must preach for a response again.

This decision involved me in the hardest inward battle I had yet experienced in these parishes. Whether I wanted it or not I was being given a crash course in spiritual warfare. As the Sunday approached I found myself increasingly nervous. I wished that I could avoid this ordeal.

I knew that this would be a new teaching to both congregations. I prayed that they would be like the Beroeans in Acts 17:11, 'examining the Scriptures to see if these things were so'. But I was afraid of trouble and division. I knew that other churches had been split by the baptism of the Spirit, and now I was about to take the first decisive step down that road wherever it might lead. But although this decision gave me the jitters, God did not permit me to hesitate or waver over it.

I believed in the baptism of the Holy Spirit as a vital

part of our redemption: in John the Baptist's words, it was what Jesus actually came to do, as important as taking away the sin of the world. I had a responsibility to declare the whole counsel of God. How could I miss this out? I knew from too many years' experience that there was no other way for the church to be renewed. All the good ideas, new forms of worship, new songs or hymns, house groups, Christian Stewardship, lay ministry—none of it was any use without the power of the Holy Spirit. To try and run a church without the power from on high, was like trying to run a car without petrol. Trying to get Christians to behave like Christians without the baptism of the Holy Spirit was like flogging a dead horse. So it had to be done and done now. Like praying for healing or calling people to a public act of commitment, it was not going to get any easier for being put off. Start as you mean to go on: I had learned that lesson now.

We had already spoken about the baptism of the Holy Spirit in the two Bible study groups. If I did not preach it publicly it would give the impression that this was something to be hidden away, almost to be ashamed of, like, say, homosexuality—only to be practised by consenting adults in private. In fact the baptism of the Holy Spirit is the rightful inheritance of every believer and should be the normal experience of Christians.

Nevertheless I was late going to sleep on the Saturday night, and awake again early on Sunday morning with a very wobbly tummy. The day started at St. George's, as usual, and I told the whole congregation the story of my own baptism in the Spirit: how I had been a Christian and how I had been ordained for many years before I discovered that there was some-

thing more. Then I said it again: 'Now I want you to
get up out of your seats, if you too want to receive what
the Father has promised. Come forward and I will lay
hands on you and pray for you to be filled with the Holy
Spirit.'

Again I came down from the pulpit and waited. At
first no one at all moved. Then a middle-aged couple
got up and came forward, and an elderly woman from
the other side of the church. No one else. So I prayed for
these three, laid hands on them, and they went back to
their places. It was in God's hands.

I went on to St. Nicholas' later in the morning and
gave the same message. Then I could hardly believe my
eyes: practically the whole congregation was getting up
again and coming forward (they must have been getting
used to it). Perhaps six people stayed in their places,
while thirty or so were crowded along the altar rail. I
called Maureen out of the congregation; she started at
one end and I at the other, and between us we laid
hands on them all and asked Jesus to baptise them with
the Holy Spirit.

It was not possible to stop and enquire what was
going on in people's minds as they came forward. How
much did they understand of what I had said? What
were their expectations as we prayed for them? Nor was
it possible at the time to stop and enquire what effect
our prayers were having upon people. Later, more of
the detail would emerge, but there and then I was
simply doing what I believed God wanted me to do,
and leaving him to do the rest.

The situation never really changes. However many
people in the church may have been filled with the
Spirit, however many dramatic and life-changing

events may have taken place, however openly charismatic the life of the church may become, to those outside it all remains a mystery until they open themselves up to the Spirit of God. Paul says that the natural man cannot understand the things of the Spirit, because we need the Spirit to discern them (1 Cor. 2:14). This is a sort of spiritual double bind: we cannot understand the Holy Spirit except by the Holy Spirit. That is why it is possible for people all through the Bible and for people today to hear and hear and not understand, to see and see and not perceive. For everyone, receiving the Holy Spirit is largely a leap in the dark; we do it not because we understand, but either out of sheer obedience to the word of God, or out of trust in the testimony of a friend, or because we have seen in other people something which we simply do not understand.

Of the three upon whom I laid hands at St. George's, all noticed the difference. Milly felt her head tingling as I touched her. She started sleeping properly at night for the first time in many years, and had an inner peace which even her daughter noticed. Of those we prayed for at St. Nicholas', some experienced physical sensations at the time and physical changes afterwards. A young father, Stuart, who had only moved to Ashill a few weeks before, found that Sunday what he had been searching for spiritually for several years, and never looked back. Others, like me, were apparently untouched by God at the time, but dramatic changes began to happen in their lives in the weeks that followed. With others, it has to be said, it seems as if the baptism of the Spirit did not work.

I do not believe that God is arbitrary or capricious. He certainly deals with us all differently, but we also come to him with different attitudes and expectations. I could not tell that Sunday morning, nor can I tell to this day, what was in the hearts of those who came forward. It is there, in the secrets of the heart, that I believe we should look for an explanation of why in some cases the baptism of the Spirit did not seem to 'take'.

However, the one positive thing that is true of them all is that not one of those who came forward that Sunday has subsequently left the congregation, though others have. The response of a few people may perhaps have seemed to make little difference, but they have generally remained supportive of what God has been doing in our churches since then. At St. George's the word about the baptism of the Spirit and the response of those few started an irritation, like a speck of gravel in an oyster, which has continued to this day but around which a pearl is slowly growing. At St. Nicholas' what happened was more like the saying 'light the blue touch-paper and retire'.

—

SEVEN

PRAY CONTINUALLY

...AND RETIRE.' There is not much else to do at such times. It is a position I often found myself in during the early days in these two parishes, and a position I have often found myself in to the present day. I did what was given to me to do: I lit the blue touch-paper, and it seemed such a small, even insignificant thing. But then there was nothing more that I could do, except wait and see what God would do next. It is a position of great expectation, but of complete helplessness—a state of total dependence on God.

And it is not a bad place to be. The natural man in me resists it: I like to be in charge, making things happen. This is the end of pride for me. But the Spirit of God loves us to be in this place of dependence, and we can learn to love it too. Over the years I have come to feel a greater sense of peace and security in this place than anywhere else. It is the true place of prayer.

I knew this place before Maureen and I ever moved to these villages. I wanted to see these two churches come alive and grow in the power of the Holy Spirit, but I knew that I could do nothing to make it happen. Only God could do it. As Maureen and I laid hands on Christine in the shop I knew that what we were doing had no power to heal her. Only God could do it. As we prayed for people in church to be baptised in the Holy Spirit I knew that I could do nothing to change anything in the spiritual lives of these parishioners. Only God could do it.

So I knew from the beginning that the most important thing to do was to pray. I had not only to pray myself but to invite and encourage others to join me in prayer. So straightaway we started a church prayer meeting in each parish. We began by meeting for just half an hour early in the evening once a month. Little enough, but it was like a post driven into the ground, a marker which would serve as a reference point for the building of the temple: ' "Not by (your) might nor by (your) power, but by my Spirit", says the Lord Almighty' (Zech.4:6).

Not many people came to the prayer meetings, perhaps six or eight in either parish, but it was enough. I tried to explain what the prayer meeting was for, how we needed to come before God in brokenness and emptiness, and cry out to him to save us and our church and our nation. We would not meet primarily to pray for personal needs, though these might find a place, but to call upon God to revive us again, to rend the heavens and come down in converting, life-changing power upon our churches, our villages, and the wider world around us.

Those who came quickly got the idea and, indeed, we discovered that God had already planted this desire in some of their hearts. But how do people sustain even half an hour of prayer? Many of us were beginners at prayer meetings. Most Anglicans are not used to praying without a book at all. Before I was baptised in the Spirit I had carried a pocket edition of the Prayer Book with me everywhere, and whenever I was called upon to pray, I would read out a collect or two suitable to the occasion. Caught without my Prayer Book I was dumb. So I understood the problem. But I did not believe that at this point God wanted a formal service read out to him month by month.

It is indeed odd when children are unable to talk naturally to their father about what is in their hearts, but can only read other people's speeches to him out of a book. Nevertheless that is where we often start from in the Church of England. It needs tact and patience to encourage God's children to find a voice of their own in which to talk to him. Even those who can talk to their Father quite easily when they are on their own, at the sink or in the car, seem to be reluctant to do so in front of others. People who pray long, clever, fluent prayers at a prayer meeting can be just as intimidating as the vicar reading out of a book.

As with so much else, I have found that these inhibitions are most effectively overcome by the baptism of the Spirit. A person who has sat mutely through many prayer meetings, lost or embarrassed at the idea of saying anything themselves, is usually released by the baptism of the Spirit, if not into an unknown tongue at least into their own. Sometimes suddenly, sometimes gradually they find they have things to say to God which they did not have before, and they begin to say them in their own words, easily and naturally. I am sure that God delights to hear this, as much as a human parent delights to hear his children's first words.

To start with, a whole meeting might pass when only Maureen and I would pray out loud. The temptation for us was to rabbit on, filling the void. But had we done so no-one else would ever have found the freedom or the courage to speak. So silence would often fall, not always an easy or prayerful silence but sometimes an awkward and fidgety silence in which people did not know what to do or say. As time went on more people found a voice, the prayers began to flow from one person to another, and the silences when they did fall became deeper silences of concentrated prayer.

Over the years these prayer meetings have grown, in various ways. After about a year the meeting at St. Nicholas' extended from half an hour to a more open-ended time, usually about an hour and a half. After two years people were saying to me, 'We aren't praying often enough.' 'Once a month is not enough; it ought to be once a week.' So the monthly prayer meetings in both parishes became weekly ones.

We have also learned more about how to structure a prayer meeting. The longer meetings start with a time of praise, often unaccompanied singing. It is right to remind ourselves of the greatness and the goodness of the God to whom we pray, and the love and power of the Lord Jesus in whose name we pray. We then usually have a reading chosen from Scripture. It is perfectly true that we do not know how to pray as we ought. It is also true that the Holy Spirit wonderfully helps us in our weakness. But perhaps the principal way in which the Spirit helps us is through the word.

In the Scriptures God has revealed to us his purpose and plan for his world and mankind. Our job is to pray that purpose into being, concentrating on that bit of the world and humanity in which God has chosen to set us. In the Scriptures God has also given us many examples of good praying, in the psalms, in the prophets, in the epistles and in the lives of Jesus and the early Christians. The Scriptures feed and direct our prayers.

Jesus promised that whenever we pray in his name—whenever, that is, we pray his prayers—we shall obtain what we ask. There can be no more certain way of praying according to God's will than to pray his word back to him. All fathers know that the most devastating request our children can bring to us is, 'Dad, you said …' I am sure that our heavenly Father loves to be reminded of his promises, because he is longing to keep them.

As time has gone on we have also found the benefits of focusing our prayers on particular aspects of the church's life and work week by week. After about three years I asked someone else to take over the leadership of this prayer ministry at St. Nicholas'. Allan, to whom the Lord has given a special gift in this field, now coordinates prayer for particular purposes each week. One week we will pray especially for the worship group, or for the house fellowships. If we pray for the Sunday school the teachers can come and bring their registers so that we can pray over each child by name, as well as for the teachers themselves. This is not to the exclusion of other concerns or more general prayers, but it has added a greater sense of purpose and responsibility to the meetings.

No one can measure the power or effectiveness of prayer. God has commanded us to pray and to ask, and we show our faithfulness by being constant in prayer. But more than any external obedience, prayer belongs to the innermost dynamics of the kingdom of God. It is God who does it. Without him we can do nothing. Prayer is a simple acknowledgement of that truth. Whatever God has done in these two villages from the beginning he has done as a result of that radical dependence on him that is called prayer.

—

EIGHT

EXPLORE THE LAND

I T WAS TIME to consolidate the bridgehead and push on into some of the new territory that baptism in the Spirit opens up. Two opportunities presented themselves.

First, I was only too aware that the people who had responded to my invitation to be filled with the Holy Spirit had very little understanding or knowledge of what I meant. Their response was probably as much a gesture of goodwill or trust in me as anything else. But there is a tradition in the Church of England that people take part in some extra Christian activity in the six weeks before Easter called Lent. Some churches may have extra midweek services, while others hold study groups. So I planned a course of Bible study for the two churches on the person and work of the Holy Spirit during Lent.

I have a tidy mind; God does not—at least not my sort of tidy. In my garden things grow where they are told, and I umpire with the secateurs and shears when plants are getting too close to each other. But I have noticed that in God's horticulture things come up higgledy-piggledy, all over the place, and grow in wild profusion. Our attitudes to spiritual growth tend to be

like this too, and I have had to learn to give way to him
time and again over how he makes things grow. I would
have liked all those people who had come forward for
the baptism of the Spirit to come to the Lent meetings
and learn more about it and I said so, to him and to
them. What God sent was a much more varied assortment, including a Methodist, one or two Baptists, a
Roman Catholic and two complete strangers. Inevit-
ably, not many people could come regularly throughout
the six weeks; people would be there one week and
away the next. In spite of it all fifteen to twenty people
turned up once a week in each parish and we looked at
what the Bible says about the Holy Spirit.

It is indeed remarkable that Jesus himself, who we
believe to be the very Son of God, did not do or say
anything that anyone found memorable before he was
filled with the Holy Spirit, at his baptism in the river
Jordan. All his unforgettable teaching and astonishing
miracles followed that. The apostles up to the Day of
Pentecost were bewildered, frightened men; after the
Spirit came, they were bold witnesses, able to understand and testify to what God was doing. We studied
this remarkable change both in the life of Jesus and in
the lives of the apostles and then went on to look more
closely at the gifts which the Spirit gives and at the fruit
of the Spirit in their lives and ours.

No one was bored; people were stirred. Not everyone
was entirely happy. Robbie met one or two other parishioners of St. Nicholas' on the village green one day
and they shared their feelings with one another. 'Well, I
don't know about this talking in tongues. It don't make
much sense to me. It may be in the Bible, but I don't
think we want it in our church. After all, we are only a
country village. What would people think of us if we all

started doing that?' (Not that anyone actually had started doing it, at least not then).

More serious reservations were surfacing in the other parish. The lay reader who had first interviewed me at St. George's had agreed to lead one of the studies, but a week before it he wrote to me declining to take any more part. 'I would have liked to have seen a good period of quiet consolidation to enable you to get to know us and vice versa,' he wrote. 'I think the many changes you have in mind will be counter-productive if put in hand too soon'.

Like Hezekiah, all I could do was to spread the letter before the Lord. I examined it and myself before his face. I did not have a programme of changes in mind, though perhaps it appeared as if I had. I sincerely believed that I was not in charge of all this anyway; the commander-in-chief who was directing this operation, including its timing, was not me. But I was not immune to a twinge of doubt: many people, even a part of me, would have said that these counsels of quietness and caution were wise. Yet the peace of Christ ruled in my heart as I reviewed the events so far.

The second opportunity that presented itself was not of my making at all. The Diocesan Renewal Fellowship had arranged a visit by Bishop David Pytches and a team from St. Andrew's, Chorleywood. They would be teaching and demonstrating how to minister in the power of the Spirit. I was thrilled, because I had learned a great deal from David Pytches myself, and this opportunity to take people from these two new parishes to hear him was a God-send.

There would be at least two aspects to this experience for them. First, people would hear the sort of teaching that I had been giving them from someone else, another Church of England vicar and a bishop to boot! They would see that I was not just a crank, or if I was, that there were others like me in the Church of England. I knew that much of what they had heard from me would be confirmed by David Pytches because I had learned it from him in the first place. It would be an introduction to the wider charismatic movement in the church.

It would also be an introduction to charismatic worship. At St. Nicholas' they had sung one or two of the new songs, but I knew they had never experienced full-blown charismatic praise and worship, hands raised and all. The dozen or so who put their names down to attend this day would be like the spies sent up from the wilderness to view the Promised Land.

This was, of course, a high-risk strategy. What if, like the spies in the Bible, they came back and said Canaan was horrible and they were certainly not going in there? A real possibility: not all churchgoers respond favourably to guitars and synthesizers, to clapping and swaying and bopping up and down. For people who have only ever experienced *Hymns Ancient and Modern* and Anglican chant there is at least a culture shock. Worse than that there is also a spiritual shock: most churchgoers seem to be unacquainted with joy. The joy of the Lord is not their strength, which is one of the reasons that the churches are so weak. Charismatic worship exudes joy. It is not a joy of the flesh, though the beat and the popular songs can engender that too. Nor is it that heartiness which comes of knowing that Christians are supposed to be joyful even when they are not. It is a joy of the spirit, the fruit of the Spirit. Yet many, more traditional worshippers who are used to solemn ceremonies and perhaps, in their hearts, used to misery, find real joy difficult to take.

Why did I worry? From the first chord Jean knew that she had found what her soul had craved all her life. Jean, the mother of two college-age children, had been a dogged and faithful supporter of St. George's ever since she had moved to the village thirteen years before. Always, as she sat through the tedious services in a nearly empty church she knew in her heart that there must be something more to it than that. She had learned more about Jesus and the forgiveness of sins through Mission England in 1984, but she had been afraid to let go and surrender her life to him. At the Day of Renewal David Pytches invited people to do just that, with the words of Jesus: 'Come to me, all you who are weary and burdened, and I will give you rest' (Matt 11:28). That was Jean. She went forward, asked Jesus to come into her life and fill her with his Spirit, which he did.

Alan, churchwarden at St. Nicholas' and headmaster of the village school, had come forward for the baptism of the Spirit, but without much expectation of anything new. It was now, some months later, that it all started to happen to him. David Pytches, as he does, invited God to send the Holy Spirit in Jesus' name. Those who felt God's anointing on them were invited to come forward, and Alan did so. He came back feeling sixty feet tall. He went on feeling sixty feet tall for the rest of the day. When he walked he felt as if he was wearing seven-league boots. Being an early and energetic riser he was up in good time the next morning and went out to spend some time in the garden before getting ready for church. After a while he felt a strong desire to go indoors again to pray, and as he did so, he started speaking in tongues.

Next Wednesday we were meeting as usual for the Lent study group. Alan told everyone what had happened to him just a few days before. Ten words of testimony are indeed worth a hundred words of argument. The Lord had confirmed the word with signs following.

NINE

—

MAKE A SANCTUARY FOR ME

MOST OF THE law of Moses consists of regulations about worship. It is there, in the latter part of the book of Exodus and in the book of Leviticus, that people who start reading the Bible at page one usually come to a grinding halt. Endless instructions about what sacrifices are to be offered, and when, and where, and by whom, and how, even down to regulations about the priests' underpants are enough to stop most people in their tracks.

The New Testament, by contrast, contains very few regulations about worship (and none at all about underpants). On the contrary Jesus cancels at a stroke all the Old Testament ceremonial laws. 'Yet a time is coming and has now come when the true worshippers will worship the Father in spirit and truth' (John 4:23). St. Augustine wrote 'In the new dispensation, our Lord Jesus Christ has knit his people together in fellowship by sacraments, which are very few in number, most easy of observance, and most excellent of significance, namely baptism solemnised in the name of the Trinity, and the communion of his Body and Blood'. After that, or around that, Christians are free to worship as together they are led in spirit and in truth.

The fact that the law of Moses is no longer binding upon us, however, does not mean that it is mere junk. The most general lesson that it still teaches us is that worship is important, even the details of worship. High up on the agenda of every church should be concern about the worship. Is the worship real? Is it a living sacrifice, or is it a bondage to some dead law, a formality, an empty shell? Are the outward forms of worship—the words, the music, the ceremonies—vehicles for the worship of the heart, or have they become impediments to that? It is worth taking a lot of time over getting the worship right. God did, and so did we.

When the church councils of St. George's and St. Nicholas' first met with me, I gave each member a piece of paper, and after praying about it, everyone wrote down the things they thought were on God's agenda for our churches. The responses were various: 'New carpets'; 'A choir or group of singers to lead the music'; 'Services which will appeal to the young'; 'Sincerity in our worship—no gimmicks'. Most of the concerns expressed were somewhere in the area of worship, so we began to look at what we were doing and why.

Church of England parishes in the countryside usually have to make do with a somewhat erratic pattern of services that depend on the vicar shooting around on Sundays officiating at different times at different places. Our two villages are relatively large, each one having a population of about 1400. So each has a main morning service every Sunday, at 9.30 a.m. at St. George's and 11.00 a.m. at St. Nicholas'.

Now any church which is more than about twenty years old (and our two churches are at least 700 years old) has had to grapple with certain basic issues about worship. Every church has either resolved those issues over the last twenty years or will have to do so over the next twenty. Most of the issues revolve around the question of the relationship of the church's worship to current culture. When a person steps through the door of a church, does that person have to step back into the culture of 100 years or 400 years ago? To be made to do that can be alienating for the great mass of the unchurched.

The first issue is that of language. Do we speak to God and about God in the language of the past or the present? Do we use the seventeenth century King James version of the Bible, or a more modern translation? When we pray, whether extempore or from a book, do we call God 'you' or 'thou'? This issue has been particularly acute in the Church of England because in the seventeenth century *Book of Common Prayer* we have one of the masterpieces of English literature. Do we abandon that for the very ordinary twentieth century words of the *Alternative Service Book?*

The second issue, possibly even more emotive, is about music. The musical tradition in most of our churches is solidly Victorian. In the last twenty years the charismatic renewal has produced a flood of new songs. But the idiom of both the words and the music is very different from the traditional one. The new songs are written to be sung to the accompaniment of guitars, keyboards and drums, not to the church organ. The words are often uncomfortably direct and personal for the churchgoer accustomed to Victorian verse.

The third issue is the place of children in the church. Should children be in church with their parents or should they be separated? If children are seen they will be heard too. Can adult worship tolerate the disturbance of children?

The fourth issue, which is related to all the others is less easy to define. How formal or informal should worship be? How much interaction between people should there be, as opposed to interaction with God? How much should be regulated and how much spontaneous? How much congregational participation should there be, and how much should be performed by professionals?

A fifth issue is how frequently or infrequently an act of worship should be focused on the breaking of the bread. This is a more perennial issue, but not the less important for that.

I did not come to St. George's and St. Nicholas' with a blueprint for worship in my mind. I had developed certain convictions over the years, but I was prepared to wait and see how and when and even whether those convictions could be worked out in these two churches. In any case we had to start from where they were, and go on from there together. And they were at very different places.

St. Nicholas' had moved along with the revision of the liturgy in the Church of England and used modern-language services with hardly a backward look. But three Sundays a month a separate Sunday school met at 10.00 a.m., and the service for adults which followed had a congregation of less than thirty. Once a month there was a Family Service where adults and children came together, and the congregation often exceeded 100. It was not difficult to see that most Sundays we were effectively discouraging families from worshipping together and even preventing parents from worshipping at all.

Change is always threatening since it is always plain what we have to lose and uncertain what we have to

gain. However, guided by the Scriptures, St. Nicholas'
church council were willing to launch out into the deep.
We noticed that in the Old and in the New Testaments
children always appear before God in the company of
their parents. We also noticed the pattern of life of the
early church, as recorded in Acts: 'They devoted themselves to the apostles' teaching and to the fellowship, to
the breaking of bread and to prayer' (Acts 2:42).

By May we were ready to inaugurate an act of worship every Sunday that involved all age groups, that
was based on the modern Communion service in the
Alternative Service Book, but that made maximum use of
the flexibility and variety allowed by that service. The
details were worked out in the church council. The
result was something which was very much our own,
adapted to what we saw as our own particular needs
and situation but still within the rubrics of the Church.
The basic ingredients of teaching and fellowship, of the
breaking of bread and of prayer have remained constant ever since, but our worship has gone on develop-
ing and changing. Like the design of a car, the main
components have stayed in place, but we have gone on
modifying the bodywork and the engineering.

St. George's started from a very different place. The
seventeenth century Book of Common Prayer still provided the words. The Victorians still provided the
music. A robed choir aimed at the sounds of a great
cathedral. Like *The Mousetrap*, a 1940s thriller still running on the London stage, the show was still playing in
the late twentieth century, though to very small houses.
Just once a month a Family Service made a gesture
towards the younger generations of parents and children but it was borne with an ill grace by many of the
older worshippers.

Against this background I discovered that the church council at St. George's was already a battle-ground, with at least three different tendencies within it, all of them militant. There were those who positively prided themselves on the traditionalism of St. George's, and there were others who were fretting for change. Those who were fretting for change were themselves, however, pulling in different directions. This was none of my doing, but I must have brought yet another dimension into their old battles. It was an unhappy situation for everyone, a recipe for strained immobility, a situation in which the Church of England only too often finds itself: like a ship tied up so tightly at both ends that it can move neither forward nor back.

We considered the possibility of splitting into two separate congregations with a traditional service and an alternative one, but rejected it. For better or worse we decided to stay and work through our differences together. I don't know whether that was the right decision or not. In the circumstances in which we found ourselves, perhaps an amicable separation would have been the better way forward. But it does strain the leadership resources in a rural situation and for that reason as much as any other we decided to follow the other course, and so we locked ourselves into an on-going battle.

We also considered the possibility of letting each village go its own way: St. Nicholas' being the 'modern' church and St. George's the 'traditional'. Apart from the fact that I believed such a distinction would be the equivalent of condemning St. George's to death, it was a very attractive option, not least to those members of St. George's who wanted to move on. The temptation has gone on recurring, but in the end villages are profoundly separate communities and it goes against the grain of village life to live in one village and worship in another. So we rejected that possibility too, and in spite of the battles and frustrations St. George's people have stayed in St. George's to fight it out.

I became aware as time went on, that the battle was ultimately a spiritual one, though it is all too easy to wrestle not with the principalities and powers but with the flesh and blood which seems to embody them. Every '—ism' is a spiritual principality: there is a spirit of Anglicanism, even a spirit of Evangelicalism and a spirit of Anglo-Catholicism within Anglicanism, just as there is a spirit of Methodism and of Pentecostalism. Our traditions, whatever they are, no less than the traditions of the Pharisees, can so easily come between us and obedience to the living God. It is the subtlest temptation of all to substitute a form of religion for God himself.

In St. George's there seemed to be an actual part of the building where such a spirit of religion reigned: the chancel, where the organ was situated and the choir sat. The choir were a varied assortment of individuals, yet time and again a division over matters of worship resolved itself into a division between the choir and the rest of the congregation. It was not just a question of personal preferences; most people were big enough to recognise the need for some give and take. It was the presence of a much more dominating spirit which said that things absolutely must be done or said or sung in a certain way.

After eighteen months of deadlock in the church council, during which the question of worship could not be settled but would not go away, we established a committee to dig deeper. The committee read a book together which put Christian worship in a broader historical and Scriptural perspective, and also recounted the experience of another church which had faced the same problems as we had.* Rather to our surprise this committee was able to produce a unanimous plan for change. Even more to our surprise this plan was adopted by a large majority of the church council. It was a miracle.

St. George's began to change. Out went the old prayer book for the main Sunday service, and in came modern language. St. George's, like St. Nicholas', became more sacramental, focusing the worship on the breaking of the bread.

The changes were not as radical as at St. Nicholas'. The feel of the service remained traditional even if the words were modern, but the log jam had been broken.

* *One Heart, One Voice*, Andrew Maries, Hodder and Stoughton (London: 1985)

TEN

HEAL THE SICK

'THERE IS NOT any point in preaching about healing the sick unless you do it.' God was speaking to me again as I prepared a sermon, this time about Jesus the healer. Of course we had already begun to do it, with people like Christine and Sue. But that was not in any public way, and I still had not begun to teach or explain about Christian healing.

This is the black hole in the life of most churches. The gospels say repeatedly and unequivocally that Jesus healed the sick, and give many detailed examples of his activity. The book of Acts says that the apostles went on doing the same thing. Jesus actually promised that thosee who believed in him would do even greater things than he had done. Yet there is very little today in the life of most of the older churches which corresponds to this.

A discrepancy such as this between the Scriptures and the life of the church today is uncomfortable. This discrepancy and others like it have given rise this century to a whole new academic industry: liberal theology. If what we read in the New Testament is so different from what we have experienced in our churches, then either we have to look for a new way of reading the Scriptures or we have to look for a new experience in our churches. The first course has led to liberal theology; the second to the charismatic renewal. Liberal theology consists of the invention of more and more sophisticated reasons for not believing what we read. The charismatic is a seeking after God to renew the New Testament experience of the church.

When challenged by the stories of the healings of Jesus the average churchgoer and indeed the average preacher is likely to respond that Jesus is alive and well and working for the National Health Service. It is to doctors and nurses and hospitals that we should look to see God at work today. That used to be my own attitude. I visited the sick and I discussed their operations, I encouraged or consoled the relatives, I read Psalm 23 and the Lord's Prayer with them. But if they got better it was through the ministrations of the doctor, not me. There had been a black hole in my ministry too.

Now I had to begin to fill in that black hole in the understanding and expectations of these two churches: the great healer in the New Testament is not Luke the physician but Jesus the miracle-worker. There are, of course, innumerable questions which crop up along the road in the Christian healing ministry. Why are some people apparently healed and others apparently not? What is the relationship between supernatural healing direct from God and natural healing through the medical profession? But it is important simply to begin. Jesus healed the sick. Jesus said to those he sent out, 'Heal the sick' (Matt. 10:8). It is more important to be obedient than to worry about the hard questions. So I announced that day in church that I believe that Jesus still heals the sick, and that he wants to use us to minister healing to one another in his name.

After the sermon the only thing left was to do it. Once again I invited people to get up out of their seats, some to seek healing for any ailment or infirmity with which they might be suffering, others to join me in laying hands on them. A third time there was a response: six people came to the altar rail for healing, and a small group gathered round behind them. As we went along the row, I encouraged the others to lay their hands on the sick while I prayed for each one.

Christine's daughter Louise was spending that weekend at home. She was carrying a baby and having some difficulty with it. She was suffering a good deal of pain and feeling quite ill six months into her pregnancy. She laid hands on her own stomach as we prayed over her. From that day on she felt fine and carried the baby for the rest of the time without trouble.

I have never planned very far ahead in these two parishes. I did not know where we should go from there. I had been to special 'healing services' to which the sick were encouraged to come especially for this ministry. But they only happened occasionally, perhaps once a month. What were you supposed to do if you were taken ill just after the healing service? Wait a month for the next one? I liked better the idea that a ministry of healing should be available at any service, or for that matter at any place, at any time—over the counter in the electrical shop, for example, or on the kitchen floor. After all, the healing ministry of Jesus was not confined to an occasional service in the synagogue. Most of his miracles of healing took place in the street, or in houses or by the sea-shore. Wherever and whenever crowds gathered to hear him, Jesus healed the sick.

I had also been to healing services where everyone lined up to receive prayer and have hands laid on them by one particularly gifted man or woman. I did not doubt that there were some people much more powerfully used by God in this way than others. They were the ones that became big names on the posters advertising the rallies and conventions. But to rely only on the ministries of such gifted people was to restrict the availability of Christian healing even more. I liked better the idea that this was something which all Spirit-filled Christians should be taught and encouraged to do. All twelve of the apostles were commanded to heal the sick, and later to teach other disciples to do the same thing. It was not of some special group of Christians that Jesus spoke when he said, 'they will place their hands on sick people, and they will get well'; it was of all those who believed in his name (Mark 16:17–18).

When the Lent meetings ended at Easter, many people did not want to stop. In particular they wanted by then to know more about both the theory and the practice of the ministry of healing. So we carried on for another four weeks after Easter. About twenty-five people continued to come, now drawn from both churches together. I taught from the Scriptures about healing and then we practised on each other.

My own wife Maureen was healed through these meetings, first of cystitis, and then of a chronic and recurring pain in the ribs. Evelyn was healed of arthritis in the thumb, Rene of tummy trouble. We also began to ask God for words of knowledge and our first tentative efforts were remarkably blessed. Alan had a revelation about someone with a bad knee. This was Stuart who had permanently damaged a cartilege playing football. He was greatly improved after we prayed for him.

At the end of this course of meetings I said I wanted to establish a healing ministry team. Both churches needed a group of people who knew something about praying for and laying hands on the sick, and who had the faith to do so. Then we could offer ministry for healing at every service, confident that there would be at least one or two people present, apart from me, who could do it. I was willing to encourage every Christian to pray for the sick in their own homes, or in the street if they dared. But what they did there was their own responsibility before God and they were answerable for it. What was done in church was my responsibility and I had to be answerable for it, not only to God but to the bishop and the parish at large. So in church people had to have my explicit authority to minister in this way.

I offered that authority to any of those who had come to and taken part in the meetings. God knew and I knew that we all had a lot to learn about the healing ministry but in this, as in most things, the most effective learning is done on the job. It was time for us all to get on with it. We prayed then, and asked God to choose those whom he wanted to be the nucleus of the healing ministry team. I asked those who felt God's calling to put up a hand while everyone kept their eyes shut. When I looked up there were exactly twelve hands up, six from each parish. There are certain things only God can do.

—

ELEVEN

YOU WILL BE HATED

ONE DAY IN JUNE I received a letter in the post. It was from our lay reader at St. George's. He regretted to tell me that he did not any longer feel able to support me, and that he would be resigning from the end of July. He had, as he said, already expressed his disagreement with me on a number of occasions, so his resignation did not come as a complete surprise. He did not want to discuss the matter any further with me, so that was that.

Six months after moving into the parish I had lost one of the key people in the church. He had been a pillar, perhaps the main pillar of St. George's. Although retired, he had been very active—especially during the vacancy between my predecessor and me—not only in preaching and leading worship, but in visiting the house-bound and infirm. I had continued to welcome his ministry, and indeed only recently I had signed the nomination papers for the renewal of his licence as a preacher. Now he was not just resigning from his ministry, but leaving the congregation altogether. And when he left would others go with him?

However, I respected his wishes and did not try to pursue the matter any further or to persuade him to change his mind. His decision had indeed been fore-shadowed; early on he had warned me about going too fast. More recently, he had made plain his disagreement with various things I had done.

He was not happy with the healing ministry. He objected in particular to two or three of the people whom I had commissioned as part of the ministry team. They did not seem to him to be suitable. But perhaps there was a deeper unease, a more general disquiet about the gifts of the Spirit. This is a phenomenon that I was to encounter at many points, not least among those who had been for many years committed to the church. Of course, the charismatic gifts are new in the experience of such long-established churchgoers: that is what the charismatic renewal is all about. But in the face of the evidence of the New Testament it is difficult to maintain that they are alien to Christianity. The renewal of the gifts of the Spirit presents the same challenge again to churchgoers: are they going to put tradition before the word of God?

However, there is sometimes an emotional as well as a rational factor underlying this problem: Christians can be afraid of the supernatural. When the disciples were at sea in a boat and Jesus came to them walking on the water, their first reaction was fear. Jesus had to reassure them: 'It is I; don't be afraid' (John 6:19–20). We have to get used to the supernatural Jesus if we are to be his disciples, and that seems to be something which some of the more traditional churchgoers find very hard to do. Like my erstwhile reader, they also find the whole thing difficult to discuss, so that the roots of these fears are not easy to discover.

Another sort of supernatural conflict lay behind another of my reader's objections. I had decided to visit all the people on the church roll in both parishes. During a conversation with a man on St. George's roll I learned quite casually that he was a Freemason. I also learned that my predecessor but one, as rector of St. George's, had also been a Freemason. I said nothing at the time, though my heart had thudded uncomfortably. But I let the matter pass.

Once at home, however, I knew that this would not do. I could not ignore the presence in the congregation of Freemasonry nor my responsibility to this particular man. I could hardly blame him for not seeing anything incompatible between Freemasonry and Christianity: he had been reassured for years by the example of clergy and even bishops that the two could be combined. Yet I had to make my own belief about Freemasonry plain to him. Like the prophet Ezekiel, I knew that if I warned him and he ignored my warning then his blood would be on his own head, but if I failed to warn him his blood would be on mine.

I first came across Freemasonry when I was an assistant curate, in the cotton towns of Lancashire. I was appalled at the grip which the Lodge could exert on the life of the church, and the trouble that the Lodge could and would stir up for anyone who tried to break that grip. I was even more appalled at the blasphemous ceremonies which apparently Christian men underwent as Freemasons, deliberately and consciously excluding the name of Jesus from their prayers. I came to believe that Freemasonry was demonic and led men into occult bondage.

So a week later I went back. I tried to approach the subject as diplomatically as I could; I tried to be gentle. But as soon as I made it plain that I believed Freemasonry to be a spiritual danger the interview was over. For the first time in my pastoral ministry I was thrown out. I was told I was narrow-minded, and told not to come back. The Freemason, of course, reciprocated by never coming to St. George's again.

I did not mention the matter to anyone, but information of some sort about this visit went round the parish. How accurate it all was I never knew, but it reached our reader.

I was in trouble on yet another count. Another person on St. George's roll was a woman of middle age who was living quite openly with a man to whom she was not married. Such a state of affairs is not of course uncommon today among the young, even in country villages. But this was within the church.

The apostle Paul is quite clear that immorality must be checked, and the *Book of Common Prayer* requires that what it quaintly calls 'open and notorious evil livers' must be disciplined. 'A little yeast works through the whole batch of dough' (1 Cor 5:6). We are not called upon to dissociate ourselves from the immoral of the world at large, but we are not to admit to our own communion and fellowship those who are flagrantly disobeying the law of God (1 Cor. 5:7–13).

So once again I went visiting with the difficult and unpleasant task of rebuking sin. How I shrink from this ministry! How much easier it is to say nothing and keep the world happy. How hard it is to say the right thing in the right way. But I sensed that in both these two matters the devil was defying me to take him on, like Goliath defying the armies of the living God.

The outcome of this was not much happier than in the first case. I was not thrown out, though I was regarded as impertinent. My relationship with this person has not completely broken down though it is still strained. There has been no repentance. This pastoral exchange also reached the ears of our reader.

To him I seemed to be going round the parish doing my best to upset the parishioners and empty the church. It was true enough that we did not have all that many worshippers to start with, and here was I driving away some of those we had. Was that my idea of building up the congregation?

No pastor finds it easy to lose people from the flock, especially if the flock is already a small one. The spectre of everyone going away rises up before him. There is a sense of failure over every one that goes. And there is no shortage of people ready to point out that every person who leaves means one contribution less in the collection. Only those with the thickest of skins do not mind the odium and bad feeling that results. But any church leader worthy of the name must be prepared to go through this particular pain barrier. Jesus knew what it was to see people turn back from following him, and Jesus knew that he had to let them go. I knew that in the end the choice was either to change the message or to let them go. I let them go.

TWELVE

SING TO THE LORD
A NEW SONG

PEOPLE HAD BEEN to the Day of Renewal. More of them had been to Pentecost Praise in a neighbouring cathedral city. Young and old had had a new experience of praise and worship. It was not just that they had discovered a whole new world of Christian music, in which the songs were lively and tuneful, but their hearts had also been touched by a new intimacy with God. Now they were beginning to say 'Why can't we do it here? Why can't we sing the new songs in our own church?'

At St. Nicholas' there was nothing to stop us. The congregation was already used to singing children's songs to the guitar, at least on Family Service Sundays. There was no choir, and Jean, who laboured valiantly to play the organ, was only too willing to be relieved. There was only one problem—no other musicians. The guitarist had been the previous rector's son. Bye-bye rector, and bye-bye son.

I asked around. I was told of another man in the village who could play the guitar, a boy who was learning the drums, and another young man who was supposed to play the keyboard. None of them came to church much, but they were all known in the village. So

I went and called on them and asked each one if he would be interested in playing in a music group in church. In one way or another each declined, and with hindsight I cannot say that I am sorry. That was the easy way to learn that God's first requirement in those who lead worship is a heart for him. The hard way to learn would have been for these people to have said yes. But we still did not have anyone to play the songs.

Alan and Sue had a daughter, Becky. Becky was sixteen and had only taken piano lessons as a child, but she was part of the fellowship and she was willing to do her best. So with Becky on the piano, we began to sing some new songs, just one or two at a time. Becky did not always play the right notes, nor did we always sing them, but God did not seem to mind. He responded to our rather feeble efforts, and often we felt his presence with us as we sang. And we prayed: we prayed that God would send us musicians.

By now, Christine's daughter Louise had moved back into the village with her husband Adrian and her baby. In the cottage next door to Louise was another young couple—another country girl, Carol, and her US Air Force husband, Al. Carol too had a baby. So Louise and Carol made friends, and one day Louise invited Carol to come to church.

Carol had had a colourful youth. She had grown up in a village about forty miles away and been taken to chapel as a child by faithful Methodist parents. In her teens she had rebelled against it all. She had stopped going to church, which she found boring. Pubs and clubs offered much more excitement. A job in the fashion trade took her abroad. Carol was fairly wild. When she found she was pregnant, she married Al and came to live in our village to be within reach of Al's air-force base.

So one Sunday there was a strange young woman in church with Louise, complete with baby. As they were going out, Louise introduced her friend and neighbour. 'I can play the guitar,' Carol said. 'Would you like me to play in church?' God said yes, she was the answer to our prayers. So I said, 'Yes, you are the answer to our prayers.' And she was.

Soon after Carol started playing, I was holding some classes for people who wanted to know more about becoming a Christian. Carol came. In these classes you were supposed to become a Christian in class six and be filled with the Holy Spirit in class seven. But at class one Carol had borrowed Dennis Bennett's book *Nine O'clock in the Morning*, and by the time she came to class two Carol could not wait any longer. 'I want what it says here,' she said. So without further ado we laid our hands on her in the front room and asked God to fill her with the power of the Spirit.

Carol started laughing. She laughed for the rest of the evening. She laughed all the way home. She found it difficult to explain to Al why she was laughing because she could not stop laughing. Carol had received the joy of the Lord. She got it in such a big way that everyone who met her found it infectious. Her parents could not get over the turn-around in their daughter's life, or how their prayers for her had been answered more than they could ask or think.

Carol's joy itself had converting power. Some years later another young mother in the village, a Malayan Chinese girl called Mihoko, gave the following testimony.

I want to thank you, Carol, for 'advertising' Jesus. It

was the happiness, gladness and love that showed on your smiling face that made me stop and wonder what it was that made you so content. When Al was so far away in the Gulf War, it was the boldness in you that made me aware of my weakness. You're always so full of confidence and courage; till now I can still see and hear you talking about Jesus, about the Holy Spirit, about GOD...I am glad that I listened when I should, asked when I did, because Jesus wasted no time at all: I opened the door, and he stepped in, and my life has changed since then. Nothing could ever stop me now, I am so pleased that I've found him!

It was joy for us all to come into church Sunday by Sunday and see Carol down at the front leading the praise on her guitar.

Soon God was to add one blessing to another. Karen started coming to church. Karen had given her life to the Lord at a Christian youth camp some years before, but since then she had drifted and had not gone on in the Christian way. Now a young wife, she was looking for a way back to God. She cried when she first came to church. People often cried when they first came to St. Nicholas'. It was not because the worship was crummy (though it often was) but because God was there. Karen made an adult commitment and was baptised in the school swimming pool. Karen also played the guitar.

After starting with nothing, God had provided within six months a pianist and two guitarists. Several people, both men and women, offered to form a singing group. Sue banded them together in a song fellowship and provided some spiritual leadership for the whole group, which, for the most part, was made up of new

Christians. Musically speaking nobody was Grade 8, and we still did not sound like Pentecost Praise in the neighbouring cathedral—but God smiled on us.

THIRTEEN

—

A HOLY KISS

S PRING CAME REMARKABLY early that year. The
first daffodils were out in the churchyard before
the end of February and a week later the black-
thorn was in flower in the village street. My own rest
days during the spring were spent in the rectory garden.
Over an acre of garden had been neglected for a year
while the rectory had stood empty. By the end of March
it was so hot that I was working without a shirt as I dug
up the twitch grass and ground elder. By Easter the
hedges and even the tall trees were in leaf.

It was during these months that we explored the
renewing power of the Holy Spirit in our Lent meetings,
and then went on to discover more about the ministry of
healing. And still the people did not want to stop. Ron,
one of the three who had first come forward at St.
George's for the baptism of the Holy Spirit, insisted
that we needed a 'holy hooly' more than just now and
then. Weekly Lent meetings became fortnightly healing
meetings,and these now transformed themselves into a
monthly praise meeting. About twenty-five of us began
to meet in one church or the other on a Thursday
evening once a month. We sang the new songs for about
half an hour, and then I would teach them something

more about life in the Spirit. They would sit and listen for anything between half an hour and an hour, and then we would pray for one another and minister to one another as people had needs.

This was truly a learning place for us all. We learnt how to minister to one another and to pray for one another. But we also learnt about charismatic worship. The most obvious and visible sign of charismatic worship is people raising their hands as they sing. It is almost a symbol of the charismatic renewal. Yet it is not an isolated phenomenon; it is only one expression of a release of inhibitions about the body. Culturally, English people are not exactly at home in the body: we seem to find the body and its functions something of an embarrassment to us. We do not have the social conventions of kissing and embracing which other European people have. We tend to be buttoned up, reserved, awkward in our bodily expressions and movements.

It is a curious fact that being filled with the Holy Spirit brings us into a new relationship with our bodies. The more demonstrative aspects of charismatic worship are one expression of that; more demonstrative ways of showing our love for each other are another. Such changes in behaviour are both spontaneous and learned. The Holy Spirit puts love in our hearts both for God and for one another, and we want to express that love through our bodies. Often the response is immediate and almost irresistible: hands fly up in worship as if under someone else's control, and arms are thrown round fellow Christians with joy. But other people start off awkwardly and shyly as they try to respond to the Spirit within them.

In any case, in any sort of a congregational setting there has to be a breaking of the ice. Our monthly praise meeting was the place where the ice was broken. This was a sympathetic environment in which people could try out moving their hands and their feet in worship, and it became commonplace for people to hug and kiss each other as we met and departed. Maureen and I had to be an example and encouragement to others. But it all quickly became second nature.

But there was still a barrier to be overcome in transplanting this freedom into the Sunday services. In any older, established church there is a presiding spirit which inhibits these things. It is not only the other worshippers, who for one reason or another have not opened their hearts to the baptism of the Holy Spirit, who prickle and frown; there is something almost tangible in the air which disapproves.

To combat this, the congregation needs to be shown the physical expressions of praise in the Bible, especially in the Psalms—the clapping and lifting up of hands, the shouting and the dancing. The congregation needs to be warned about the example of Michal, who looked on and despised the liberty of David (2 Sam. 6:16–23). After that, the congregation just has to do it! Concerning the lifting up of hands in praise, Jack Taylor writes:

> This exercise is one of the most explosive and meaningful expressions of praise. I believe that God loves it, the flesh hates it, and the devil is devastated by it. I believe that with its exercise faith stands firm, fear takes flight, and joy takes hold. (*The Hallelujah Factor* Jack Taylor, Highland Books, 1985).

Spirit-filled Christians still sometimes hold back out of a false consideration for the feelings of others. It is true that other members of the congregation may be embarrassed, but it is good that they should be: it is the embarrassment of being confronted by a challenge they have not yet met. People should indeed be spared the embarrassment of having to do things which are not natural to them. Freedom in the congregation should mean freedom to lift up hands or not to lift them up, to embrace or not to be embraced, as the case may be. There is nothing more dispiriting than to see people feeling obliged to lift up their hands without the Spirit, in order to conform, and nothing sadder than to see people pushing themselves into a physical intimacy with others which does not come from the heart. We certainly need to respect the feelings and reservations of other people, and sometimes show our love for them by refraining from touching them, but we should not allow ourselves to fall back into slavery to the same inhibitions.

So, bit by bit, we took our new freedom in the Spirit back into our Sunday worship. It was easier, of course, at St. Nicholas' than at St. George's. Even at St. George's a few of us would defy the principalities and powers by raising our hands during a hymn of praise, and we incorporated the sharing of peace with each other when the modern liturgy was introduced two years after my arrival. Many and varied were the responses to this invitation to greet one another in peace: some simply refused to greet or acknowledge their neighbours in church at all, some exchanged a frigid or timid handshake; while those who had found out how to do these things kissed and hugged each other. At St. Nicholas' we watched the hands creep up—first to shoulder, then to head height, then, as the boldness came, to full stretch. The first time I said, 'Let us offer one another a sign of peace', I stood open mouthed as the congregation spontaneously became a mêlée of hugging, kissing people.

Some people have excused themselves from such demonstrative signs of love for God and one another by saying that they are English and too reserved. I appreciate the truth of that, but it misses the point. We are all English (or almost all), and once we were all reserved. Our new behaviour is the result of the work of the Holy Spirit in us. God has brought about a new integration of body, mind and spirit. The physical expressions which we are now freed to make, whether of praise or affection, strengthen our relationships both with God and with one another.

Some people regard these manifestations as mere froth, but I believe they are part of a deep process of healing. It is no wonder the English lavish such love on dogs and cats, since they do not know how to show love for one another. Many English people, not least the single and the elderly, are starved of touch. Babies that are starved of touch sicken and die; so do grown up people, inside. These expressions of charismatic worship and fellowship are life-giving. They come from the Holy Spirit, who is the Lord and giver of life.

There is, of course, a danger in all this touching and kissing: the arousal of unwanted sexual desires. This seems to have been a danger even in the days of the New Testament (Jude 4,12), and there have been too many scandals of sexual immorality concerning Christians—from high-profile television evangelists to local vicars—to pretend that the danger does not exist today. People need to be taught two safeguards. The first is that expressions of Christian love should be public, not private. Hug each other and kiss each other when other people are around; avoid such touching in private. The other safeguard is not to linger. There is no way in which this can be measured on a watch, but we know when an arm has been round the shoulders long enough. Then it is time to move away.

The possibility of a holy kiss becoming unholy should not, however, prevent such wholesome expressions of love in the first place. That would mean being ruled by fear rather than by faith. The world needs to be shown a sort of love that is warm and real, but not sexual. Our generation in particular is totally confused about sex and love, equating the two. Part of the gospel which the church has to bring to this world is of a love which satisfies our deepest needs but which does not involve sex.

Most Christians have heard that the Greek language, in which the New Testament was written, used three separate words for love. There was *eros*, which meant sexual love and passion. There was *philia*, which meant ordinary natural friendship with people we like. And there was *agapé*, a word rarely used in secular Greek writings but used throughout the New Testament to describe the love of God and the love Christians have for one another. It is the Holy Spirit who fills our hearts with *agapé*, a love for one another which is not merely an attraction towards people we like, which indeed enables us to embrace people we do not naturally like, and which is not sexual. Without being naive or imprudent with one another we need to foster and build up this love, with holy hugs and holy kisses.

FOURTEEN

—

THEY WENT AWAY

ONE OF THE growth industries in the churches of England in the 1980s was that of Christian holiday camps. Led by Spring Harvest, the doyen of them all, other holiday-cum-conference weeks mushroomed all over the country. Many a church has been nourished by these, and some have been turned upside down because members have been away to such a gathering and come back with a new vision.

David Pytches had already featured in the life of our two churches, so when he and the team from Chorleywood advertised a holiday week called New Wine, I suggested to the parishioners that a group of us might go. Since then a party of us has been to New Wine in August every year, and the party has grown to over forty. Each year this has proved to be a life-changing event for someone or other, and the experience of camping and caravanning together and eating and living in close proximity to one another has created deep bonds of friendship.

That first year there were just nine of us—two from St. Nicholas', five from St. George's, Maureen and me. We went to seminars and Bible readings in the mornings and we worshipped, more than most of us had ever worshipped before, in the evenings. On no-one did the week make a deeper impact than Jean.

Jean had been with us to the Day of Renewal earlier in the year and that had been a transforming experience for her. Much more in fact had happened to Jean that day than any of us knew till long afterwards. At New Wine Jean cried. It seemed to increase as the week went on: sometimes Jean would cry during the worship at the beginning—tender, intimate worship led by a Vineyard pastor from the United States—sometimes Jean would cry during the time of prayer and ministry afterwards. No-one knew why Jean was crying. We asked her if she was alright and she said she was. Someone sat beside her and sometimes put a comforting arm round her, but most of the time we just let her cry, trusting that God knew what he was doing even if we did not.

It was some weeks afterwards before Jean could explain. Unknown to anyone, she had been a manic-depressive for nearly thirty years. Moods of black despair and unbearable depression had alternated with times of whirling, uncontrollable mental activity. Her illness had first been diagnosed following two suicide attempts at the age of twenty-one. She had dropped out of college, unable to cope. In spite of this she had later met and married John and had brought up two children. For years she had been stabilised by heavy doses of lithium salts and anti-depressants prescribed by the doctor. She alone had been conscious of the whirling or the despair in her mind. She had successfully concealed her misery from the rest of the world.

At the Day of Renewal something changed. She did not receive any prayer for healing but the Holy Spirit coming in and filling her soul gave her a new centre of peace. She knew with such certainty that God had reached right into her with his wholeness that she went home and flushed all her medicines down the lavatory. Later, unaware of what Jean had already done and, indeed, still unaware of Jean's problem, I had taught the healing ministry team never to advise people to throw away their medicines. But Jean had done it on her own initiative and without any prompting from anyone.

In fact, she went on experiencing many of the symptoms of manic-depression. The difference was that now there was a sort of secret place within her which was no longer affected. The tempests might still roar without, but now there was a place deep within where the peace of God reigned. Jean knew that God was healing her. She told the doctor that she had stopped taking her pills. He supposed, of course, that this was just part of the manic phase of her illness. He would always prescribe for her again, he assured her, when she needed them. Jean knew she would not.

At New Wine God did more. One of the addresses focused on our need not only to be forgiven, but to forgive anyone who has hurt us. God immediately brought back to Jean's mind some very painful memories from the past. While still at college she had fallen in love with another student and they had become engaged. But her fiancé's mother took a violent dislike to Jean and broke up their relationship. Jean was not good enough for her son, and she rubbed it in at every opportunity. Eventually the boy, caught between his girlfriend and his mother, caved in and finished with Jean. Jean cracked up, tried to commit suicide and dropped out of college.

During the week at New Wine, Jean came to a place where she could forgive both her one-time fiancé and his mother for all the damage they had done to her. On the final night of the holiday she asked Jesus to heal her hurt and give her his peace. Suddenly she felt herself being bathed in lovely warm water, flooding through her whole body from top to toe, washing and cleaning every part of her.

All we had seen on the outside were Jean's tears, tears first of pain and grief, tears later of peace and joy, lots of lovely tears. But inside God had been doing his wonderful healing work. Some weeks later, at her own request and with great courage, Jean told her story in church. It is difficult to say what amazed the congregation more: the history of Jean's manic-depression or its wonderful cure.

But there was still more to come.

Jean had had an unhappy childhood. Her parents had been loving and caring enough towards her; she had never suffered any abuse; but her parents had had a wretched relationship with each other. Jean's childhood had been punctuated by her parents' violent quarrels; she was frightened by the shouting and hated what her father did to her mother. After New Wine Jean worked hard at forgiving her mother and father, especially her father, though both had by this time been dead for some years. But two years later Jean began to experience the first symptoms of the menopause. However, instead of the customary hot flushes she began to have sudden, irrational attacks of panic, and she felt the clouds of depression returning. The doctor prescribed more pills, this time hormone replacement therapy. Once again Jean kept this to herself.

After three months of this treatment, Jean knew in her heart that she was not tackling this the right way. We went again to the annual diocesan Day of Renewal, three years now since Jean's first. She went forward again at the end, this time to seek God's help with her menopausal symptoms and fears. To her amazement those ministering to her discerned the presence of an evil spirit in her, and they began to drive it out in Jesus' name. Jean fell to the ground and felt a heaving down in her bowels which came up into her stomach and then on up into her throat with a physical feeling of being sick. It stuck in her throat, but as those round her continued to pray, she coughed and coughed, and was free. We took her home, a little shaken and dazed, but conscious that something had finally gone.

Still the tale was not ended. The following morning at church Jean damaged her back carrying a heavy box. By the afternoon she was flat on her back in bed. Trying to get out of bed and move across the room she fell and hit her head on the furniture. When Maureen and I went to see her in hospital, she was recovering from concussion, but still immobilised with a slipped disc and in considerable pain. We talked first about her deliverance.

'I can confirm in my own spirit,' I said, 'that that was a demon you were delivered from. But the question is, where did it get in?'

At once God took Jean's memory back to a time when she was twelve years old. Her parents had been shouting and fighting over the meal table. The child Jean had picked up a knife and held it to her throat.

'If you don't stop it,' she had screamed at them, 'I'm going to kill myself.'

'But they didn't, and I didn't,' Jean concluded to us, and she sobbed again at the memory of it all. That was when the evil spirit had come in.

We prayed with her, asking Jesus to heal that memory, and her back as well.

About thirty-six hours later, early in the morning, Jean was praying in her hospital bed when she felt Jesus himself come and lay his hands on the back she was lying on. Her pain went, and later that day she was discharged from hospital, the doctor telling her that she had made a remarkable recovery.

God had done it all. Her back was healed; the panic attacks stopped; the hormone pills went the same way as the lithium. After returning home and while convalescing, Jean discovered one morning that for the first time in her life there was love in her heart for her parents, and she felt that she could say to both her mother and father, 'I love you'.

Jean is a new woman. Those of us who have known her have seen her change, bit by bit. We can see the new peace in her face; her eyes are calmer and her face more open. Her doctor now recognises her as cured, and even the life assurance company acknowledges her healing. Every morning Jean wakes up singing, always a song of praise and love to Jesus.

FIFTEEN

IN SEASON AND OUT
OF SEASON

'RON, I BAPTISE YOU in the name of the Father, and of the Son, and of the Holy Spirit, Amen.' Ron disappeared under the waters of the school swimming pool and came up dripping and gasping. It was June, but the water was freezing cold. I began to understand why the practice of baptism by immersion had died out in these Northern latitudes. Nevertheless, I was sure that baptism meant immersion and that the ceremony was much more memorable and significant to everyone if it was done in that way. So Ron had agreed to be baptised properly, and a small congregation was standing on the side of the pool singing as Ron and I climbed out.

More and more people have been growing up in Britain without being baptised as infants. So when they come to believe in Jesus they have to be baptised as adults. Ron was the first from our two villages to be baptised by immersion, but there have been more every year. Now, such occasions have become a regular feature of the life of our two churches.

Not that I have any objections to the baptism of infants, at least the infants of believing parents. There is a heavy prejudice in many charismatic circles against infant baptism; it is often taken for granted that the practice is unscriptural and indefensible. The fact is that there is no unambiguous statement on the subject either way in the New Testament. But after weighing the texts and the evidence as carefully as I can, I am fully persuaded myself that the apostles baptised the children of believers from the day of Pentecost onwards (Acts 2:39). I have been quite happy to follow in their footsteps.

The problem with every older denomination of the church is that of nominal or fringe membership. This is a much wider problem than that of baptism, but it is particularly acute when it comes to the baptism of the babies of only vaguely believing parents. A negative approach, that of simply discouraging such requests, does not achieve anything and flat refusal of baptism is forbidden to a minister of the Church of England. It seems better to regard such parents as simply under-evangelised, and so their children's baptism is an opportunity to share with them the good news of Jesus. Several meetings of such 'preparation' is enough to weed out those whose motives are purely worldly. Of the rest some respond more fully than others.

The couples who come to church to be married have to be regarded in a similar light. Most of them are a long way from the kingdom of God when they first come—so far, indeed, that many of them are already living together, oblivious of the fact that this is not a Christian way of life. However, unlike many of their contemporaries, they are planning to get married and in that resolution they need to be encouraged. Preparing such couples for marriage is another opportunity to explain the Christian gospel to people who are otherwise far off.

As a Church of England minister, I personally have not found the requirement to marry all that come as difficult as the requirement to baptise all babies. Marriage, after all, belongs to the order of creation rather than the order of redemption. To marry at all is to fulfil God's purpose for our nature. Couples who marry in church are not required to make statements that they do not believe; the vast majority embark on marriage in good faith. I have used the opportunity of a church wedding to encourage them to believe in marriage as the revealed plan of God for men and women, and to point them to the source of help which we all need to fulfil that plan.

Curiously, I have had most problems with giving all the dead a Christian burial. No one is obliged to have a baby baptised, and an increasing number of people do not, but every dead person has to be buried or cremated. For marriage there is a reasonable secular alternative, and many more people have been taking it, but for the burial of the dead there is virtually no decent secular ceremony. So practically all funerals are Christian ones. For me, that has been a real problem, because I do not think that most of the people I have had to bury have either lived or died as Christians, and some of them have not even pretended to do so.

The Anglican Reformers in the sixteenth century were aware of this dilemma, and the old prayer book contains a rather bleak burial service in which nothing at all is said about the dead person, and only a rather wan hope is expressed that they rest in Christ. The modern service book contains a much more positively

Christian funeral service, and the minister today is expected to speak about the deceased. And that is where the trouble starts.

The very fact of giving a person a Christian funeral at all carries a presumption that that person was a Christian and that they can be expected to inherit the Christian hope. If virtually everyone is buried in this way, as they are, it is not surprising that there is a common assumption that everyone in England is a Christian and that we are all going to the same place in the end. How then do we avoid conveying a totally false message at a funeral? How do we avoid telling lies, either implicitly or explicitly, about the dead person? At the same time, how do we avoid making judgements which no human being is in a position to make? And how do we avoid hurting and distressing relatives who are already in a state of shock and grief? What can be said on such an occasion that is not of dubious or false comfort? How does the minister preserve his own integrity, the integrity of the dead, and the integrity of the gospel?

From the first funerals I conducted in St. George's and St. Nicholas' I applied roughly the same solution to this dilemma. I said what good I could find to say about the deceased. This usually meant relying on the testimony of the family, indeed not always very reliable at such times. I tried to stick to the facts rather than employ anyone's judgement of character; God alone knows that in any case. I gave thanks to God in the funeral service for all that I could discover that was good and lovely and admirable about that person's life.

Such a eulogy alone, however, gives an unavoidable impression that we are commending the departed person to God on the basis of what he has done. Scripture passes a much more negative judgement on us: '...all have sinned and fall short of the glory of God' (Rom 3:23); and '...there is no-one righteous, not even one' (Rom 3:10). So from the beginning I said this too, and I pointed everyone to our only hope, which lies in the death and resurrection of Jesus. We do not go to heaven on account of what we have done, but on account of what he has done for us. It is Jesus who takes away our sin and offers us eternal life as the reward, not of our goodness, but of his sufferings. In most cases I have refrained from giving any indication of whether such a faith was shared by the dead person; in most cases I do not know.

In such relatively small communities as ours there are not many births, marriages or deaths in the course of a year, and it took some time for the reaction to my funeral addresses to build up. But after two or three at St. Nicholas' in quick succession in the autumn the village was seething with indignation. Whatever I had said, people had heard that the dear departed had not gone to heaven. It was apparently disgraceful that I should have said that the dead person had been a sinner.

Christine, in the electrical shop, was spending more time trying to explain the Christian faith to angry villagers than she was selling light bulbs to them. In the Post Office and by the village green groups of people gossiped about this terrible rector. But never was there such an opportunity for the church people to explain the good news of the forgiveness of sins, and many of them took it up. The comfortable clichés of folk religion had been called into question, and the village buzzed like a disturbed hive of bees.

In the end it all died down again. There was a period

of about a year when an unusual number of funerals went straight to the crematorium to be conducted by the duty chaplain. An undertaker was even asked if someone else could come and take a funeral in my church. Anything rather than have it said that we are all sinners, lost without the blood of Jesus. Bit by bit, though, the dead came back to church. People began to see that everyone got the same treatment, the church-goers as well as the non-churchgoers. Perhaps people actually started to listen to what was being said.

It was not a comfortable time while it lasted. I did not enjoy being hated. But, as with Paul's imprisonment, what happened really served to advance the gospel. From whatever motive, Christ was talked about and many of the Christians were encouraged to speak the word of God boldly. So Jesus was exalted and believers were strengthened as they stood up for the gospel.

SIXTEEN

—

FROM HOUSE TO HOUSE

THE ESSENCE OF a village, to my mind, is that everyone knows everyone else. That was certainly the case in the traditional English village in the past. In particular, it was the parson's job to know everyone and this he did by visiting everyone, whether they came to church or not. In the heyday of the English country parish the parson could carry out such a visitation at least once a year, and still have ample time left for playing tennis with his daughters and drinking tea on the lawns of neighbouring vicarages. That was the life of the English country clergy in the earlier part of this century.

Even in my own previous parishes I had managed to keep up this tradition, that is, the tradition of visiting (the tennis courts went long ago). Over the course of a few years I had assiduously visited every house in our group of villages, and made the acquaintance of all their inhabitants. In doing so I had been living up not only to my own expectations and the expectations of my predecessors, but to the expectations of many of the villagers as well. Over many a cup of tea I had been regaled with reminiscences of previous vicars, some of whom had been saints because they visited everyone, and some of whom had not because they did not.

When I arrived at St. Nicholas' and St. George's I realised from the start that expectations of that sort were now out of the question. The County Structure Plan had allowed these two villages to grow. Small estates of modern bungalows had been built for people retiring from the metropolis, and many a gap between the old cottages had been filled in with bijou residences over the previous twenty years. Now there were over six hundred houses in each village. Consciously I had to renounce my own expectations and also the expectations of the older parishioners that I would be able to visit and to know them all.

For the first year I was busy visiting those who had some sort of active connection with the two churches. We might meet frequently at church on Sundays or at various meetings in the week, but only by going into their homes could I really get to know them, their backgrounds, their families and something of their stories, especially the story of their relationship with God. While doing this I came to realise something else, something that many pastors of urban and suburban churches have also realised: that there were too many people even in the two congregations for me to keep in touch effectively with them all. Taken together there were probably between 150 and 200 people who worshipped more or less regularly. If someone were absent for two or three months would I notice it? Were they ill? Were they in trouble? Was something wrong in their relationship with God or with other people? Would I know?

I wanted the churches to grow; I expected them to grow since growth is the natural activity for a healthy church; something is wrong if a church does not grow. But one of the things that easily goes wrong in a growing church is that nobody notices when people fall away. Then, whatever is gained by mission is lost by omission. It was not too soon to start replacing the old pattern of pastoral care in these country parishes with a new one, and it was not too soon to start building a structure for growth.

House groups had been in vogue in suburban churches for at least thirty years, but they had tended to be intellectual discussion groups, places for people to share their ideas rather than places for people to share themselves. For that reason they had never really become popular in most inner city parishes or, for that matter, most rural ones. My own previous experience with rural house groups had not been very successful. But that was the only way that I could see of creating a structure for growth and pastoral care.

The House Churches had grown out of house fellowships and most of them still retained the house group as a primary cell. There was already a Bible study group in each parish here which met in somebody's house, and in St. Nicholas' there were also two or three small prayer groups surviving from Mission England several years before. These seemed to be the natural starting point. So at St. Nicholas' I gathered together the leaders of these various groups and outlined the way in which I foresaw house fellowships fulfilling the basic need for the church to provide each of its members with pastoral care.

At first I suggested that the village be divided geographically into areas, with each area being covered by its own neighbourhood house fellowship. But, as with so many other things, I later had to accept that God's mind was not as tidy as mine. The idea of the house groups was generally welcome, but for all sorts of reasons people wanted to belong to one which met in another part of the village. Rather than insist on imposing my own order on God and other people, I decided to let it happen the way it would, and six house meetings quickly got off the ground.

I did not try to prescribe what they should do when they met. I recommended prayer. Some of them were starting out from the nucleus of an existing prayer group anyway and they were happy to make that the focus of their meetings, but all of them included prayer somewhere. I recommended Bible study, but left them to decide what to study and how. For some of the groups Bible study became an important ingredient of their meetings, while others did not study the Bible together at all. I recommended that each fellowship should meet not less than once a month. Some decided to meet weekly, others fortnightly, others monthly. Compared to the tight little ship that I knew other churches ran, I realised that this all seemed very lax and untidy. For me, it was another exercise in letting God do it his way.

Each group had a Spirit-filled leader who I reckoned was able to hear from God for themselves about where their groups should go. Everyone in the church was invited and encouraged to join a house fellowship and contribute to it, but no one was coerced. People on the church roll who did not actually want to join were nevertheless allocated to one fellowship or another for the purposes of pastoral care. So each group had a pastoral list: each list consisted of the members of the fellowship and certain other members of the congregation, and it was the responsibility of the house fellowship corporately to keep in touch with each one. As new people were converted or came to the church they were encouraged to join a fellowship or were added to someone's pastoral list.

From time to time the house fellowship leaders have met together with me and we have discussed the scheme, what each group was doing, and how they were all getting on. The one thing a group is not free to do is simply to wind itself up. The house fellowships are indispensable; the pastoral life of the church depends on them.

Since they started, the house fellowships have grown and changed and divided. They have increased in number to eleven, including two youth fellowships, another one for mothers and toddlers and yet another for men. Just to convince me that God can do it better than I can, these last two—the mothers' and fathers' fellowships—were not my idea at all. God spoke to Carol about a fellowship for the young mothers, and to Stuart about one for the young men. They started them up, and God blessed them. Through them, more than any of the other house fellowships, God has brought new people to a living faith and changed lives.

Red-haired Daphne had lived all her life in the village, and gone to Sunday School as a child. She was an unmarried mum with three small children. Penny invited her to come to the young mothers' fellowship which met once a week between lunch time and coming-out-of-school time. Daphne came rather shyly, but after a few weeks she found a new relationship with Jesus and was baptised in the Holy Spirit. She started reading the Bible and, instead of walking round the village with her head down, started to smile at everyone she saw. Plenty of people noticed the difference. As for Daphne herself, she said, 'For the first time in my life, I feel I've got friends of my own.'

The life of the earliest church in Jerusalem was focused in two places, the temple where all the Christians could meet together, and their homes where they broke bread (Acts 2:46 and Acts 5:42). We have confirmed once again that the Holy Spirit likes to work in these two ways: in the congregation at church and in the more personal relationships of the fellowship in the home.

I still visit people at home. But I have escaped from the bondage which the Church of England likes to put itself under of feeling responsible for everyone who lives in the parish. I now know that pastoral responsibility is something being shared by many other Christians in the church, some of whom are far more gifted pastors than I am but who would not call themselves that. I also know that my job is to visit where I am particularly needed, with those in whose lives God himself is at work—to see what he is doing in the villages and to be there to bless it. Being the Church of England rector does give me a peculiar freedom, which I still appreciate and value, to minister to anyone in the parish, but I have shaken off the burden of trying to minister to everyone. Only God can do that.

SEVENTEEN

DIFFERENT KINDS OF GIFTS

O NE DAY GOD decided to attend the service at a
certain church. He came in as the people were
singing the first hymn. Being polite, like most
English church people, they took no notice of him. They
were encouraging one another in the hymn to praise
God. God thought that was fine.

When they finished they all sat down and a man at
the front started to talk to God. God noticed that he was
dressed up in some very peculiar clothes. God did not
understand why he had to be dressed in a funny outfit
to talk to him, but there did not seem to be any great
harm in it. Then the people were all telling him that
they had sinned. God knew that, but he also knew that
it was an important part of their reconciliation to
acknowledge it, so he was pleased. Then they stood up
to sing to him again.

As they were finishing, God was about to say how
pleased he was to be with them and how much he loved
them, but before he could open his mouth someone was
reading from the Bible. Some fine passages from the
Scriptures were read (God distinctly remembered
inspiring them) and there was one verse which God
knew was especially important for some of them to

hear. He was going to point it out, but before he could do so they were singing again.

God could feel that some of the people really loved him and had words of praise and adoration filling their hearts. But they did not have any opportunity to say them because the man in the funny outfit said, 'Let us pray'. He then prayed a long prayer about the needs of the church and the world: he mentioned the names of several church members who were ill and asked God to heal them. God longed to point out that in the congregation there was a lady with a splitting headache in the back row and a man who was terrified that he had cancer. But again, God did not get a chance to speak.

So it went on, and soon they were singing the final hymn and trooping out of the church on their way home to Sunday lunch. 'Very nice service,' they were saying to the man in the funny outfit as they left. Next week God decided not to go to that church, and he did not. Nobody noticed.

That could be any church of the historic denominations. The apostolic churches may have had liturgical forms—the Jews certainly did, since some of the forms are traceable in Scripture—but there was freedom. It was a freedom for everyone in the congregation to participate, but more importantly it was a freedom for God himself to intervene. 'When you come together, everyone has a hymn, or a word of instruction, a revelation, a tongue or an interpretation...You can all prophesy in turn...' only '...everything should be done in a fitting and orderly way' (1 Cor 14:26,31,40). Early Christian worship seems to have been characterised by freedom within a structure of order. Too often now we have the order and the structure but not the freedom.

Our monthly praise meeting on a Thursday evening once again became a learning place. I had talked at different times about the gifts of the Spirit, we had studied our Bibles and many people had read books which described the meaning and use of the charismatic gifts. Not a few people by now had received the gift of tongues in private prayer. Eighty-year-old Evelyn had been saying her prayers by the fire one November evening when, without warning, she found a torrent of unknown words pouring from her lips. She was a little alarmed and asked me about it the following Sunday. I was pleased to inform her that there was no cause for alarm: she had simply received the gift of tongues as on the day of Pentecost. 'Use it,' I told her, 'especially in your private prayers.'

But once again there was ice to break before the gifts could be expressed in a public way. So one Thursday evening, after a song and a prayer, I spoke about some of the ways in which spiritual gifts can be used in the course of worship. I then explicitly gave permission, to God and to the people, to move in the gifts of the Spirit. We then began to sing and to worship God. At one point I felt that Jean should sing and as I invited her to do so, a beautiful song in an unknown language poured out. We all listened, spell-bound and blessed. After that two other people spoke in tongues and there was an interpretation of each one. Then Stuart prophesied, fluently and powerfully, and Susan had a word of reassurance for someone who was feeling uncomfortable with it all. The ice was broken.

For most people this was their first experience of hearing the gifts of the Spirit. Later we would all have to learn lessons about mistaking and misusing the gifts of the Spirit: mistaking our own imagination for the gift of knowledge; misunderstanding or misapplying the gift of prophecy; and misinterpreting that most obscure of gifts, the gift of tongues. But on this first occasion there was something naive and genuine and unforced about these things that was beautiful.

The next step again was to introduce this element of freedom into the Sunday services. There were various obstacles. At St. George's the number of Christians who knew about or even wanted to know about the freedom of the Spirit was still relatively small. All this time the services were still being taken from the seventeenth century *Book of Common Prayer*, which does not provide many openings for speaking in tongues. In St. George's such developments would have to wait.

At St. Nicholas' more was possible. The service already included an extended time of praise and worship. We could make space here, between the songs, for spontaneous expressions of praise from anyone in the congregation, either in our own language or in tongues, or we could invite God to speak to us in prophetic utterances. Later on in the service, when we invited people to come to the front of the church for personal ministry, we could ask God to reveal what needs there were in words of knowledge, or to speak to those needs in words of prophecy.

Once again I began by explaining to the whole congregation the ways in which God could move and speak to us in the service if we would let him, and how we could find more freedom within the framework of our liturgy to offer him our own praise and adoration. Then there was nothing left but to do it, to leave gaping holes of silence and emptiness in our services and hope God would fill them with something of his own.

Sometimes he did, and sometimes he did not. Slowly

people began to feel confident enough to speak out. For all of us this was an entirely new experience. For some in the congregation there was uneasiness and embarrassment, for one or two an extraordinary fear.

One of our first words of knowledge was about someone for whom this whole business of waiting on God was traumatic, taking her back to childhood. This word was to bring Sandra to a new wholeness in her spiritual life. God had spoken to her in church one day when she was eleven years old, and she had closed her ears to his voice. Now, many years later, she found herself frightened of meeting with this same God again; but then she found that God was telling someone else, in a spirit of gentleness, that he knew of her fear. She was able to open up the whole story to God and to one or two friends, who prayed with her after the service.

Not all of the words that we have shared with one another have been so obviously or immediately fruitful. Some of them may have been from us, rather than from God. We are only learners (disciples is the Scriptural word for it), and rather slow learners at that. But we have continued to have evidence that God uses our willingness to speak and act for him. The gifts of the Spirit seem to be God's tin-openers, which he uses to open people up to him. Where there is freedom in worship for God to move, there is also a sense of excitement: something might happen. And as we now wait on him in expectation week by week, it often does.

EIGHTEEN

HIS DWELLINGS SHALL BE GLORIOUS

T HE TWO VISITORS peered through the cloud of dust. Brian, a local builder, was hacking old plaster off the tower walls and digging deep holes in the masonry with a cold chisel. The dust filled the church from end to end and the sun created great shafts of light in the haze. In a county famous for its old churches ours were not especially glorious, yet through the summer we would often discover tourists and holidaymakers walking quietly round them, savouring whatever it is that people find to savour in country churches. These particular visitors were obviously surprised and shocked to find St. Nicholas' filled with noise and dirt.

'What's going on here?' they asked the first person they met, who happened to be Christine.

'The Lord is having his house modernised,' Christine explained, and offered to show them round.

My predecessor as rector had had a vision of reordering the church and adapting the old fabric to modern usage. So the old chancel had been closed off with a glass screen, and carpeted and furnished as a separate meeting room. A platform had been built in front of the screen on which now stood a nave altar. There were more plans to convert the old vestry into a kitchen in order to enlarge the scope of the meeting room, and to install a lavatory for the greater comfort and convenience of all. But these last ideas had so far proved beyond the means of the parish. The toilet facilities had seemed to require building out beyond the existing walls, and both water and sewerage had to be brought up from the main road. It all seemed too costly and so the plans had been shelved some years before.

Then all of a sudden, without any further thought or prayer on our part, both the solutions and the money to proceed had appeared. A family of bell-ringers moved into the village, and Roger asked if he could look at the church's bells. There was a ring of six bells in the tower but they had been silent for twenty-five years because the architect had declared that the bell frame was unsafe. Roger reckoned that there was nothing wrong that could not fairly easily be put right, and set about doing it himself. When we invited the architect to come and see what Roger had done, he was satisfied that the bells could now be rung safely. So on Easter Day the bells of St. Nicholas' peeled joyfully over the village for the first time in a quarter of a century.

Everyone was thrilled, but it seemed that we now had a new problem. The tower had been earmarked to become the new vestry; now it was being used again for bell-ringing. But with the problem came the solution: put in a new floor half way up the tower. Let the bell-ringers go upstairs, and use the new room underneath as a vestry. At the back of this new vestry a lavatory could be installed, and with suitable sound insulation there would no longer be any need to build out into the churchyard.

Then a member of the church had an unusual windfall and offered £500 to pay for the water to be laid on from the road. We approached the Water Board and found that £500 would cover the cost if we moved fast; in three months the rules would be changed with the privatisation of water, and connecting the church to the mains would cost a lot more.

So, without knowing quite how far the existing funds would stretch, we set the whole scheme in motion. With Brian the local builder to do the difficult bits, Alan, a very handy churchwarden, and plenty of volunteers, the work began. Trenches were dug in the churchyard for water and mains drainage to be brought into the church. Brian started to hack into the walls of the tower to take the joists for the new floor, and at this point Christine had to explain to our visitors the story of what was going on.

The work progressed all through the summer. At one point we were about to decide that we could not afford to install the kitchen itself in the old vestry. But at that very moment a cheque arrived out of the blue from the United States for £500. It was an offering from a niece in America to thank God for the life of her uncle who had died in our village a couple of years before. And it was enough to pay for the kitchen!

While all this was going on, it came to light that the old wiring, which had been installed when the church was first electrified before the Second World War, was dangerous. In for a penny, in for a pound. We commissioned John, the other churchwarden who kept the electrical shop, to rewire the church at the same time.

After so many holes had been knocked in the walls, not to mention all the dust and the dirt, we faced a considerable amount of consequential redecoration. In fact we decided that while we were at it, the whole church could do with redecoration. We bought the tubs of traditional limewash, and through the summer holidays working parties of parishioners climbed ladders and painted the nave and the tower from top to bottom and end to end. To complete the effect, another member of the church offered to give a complete set of new carpets in pale green.

At the beginning of the year we had had just over £2000 sitting in the building fund waiting for a scheme we did not expect to be able to afford. By the end of the year we had done far more than had originally been envisaged, spent nearly £7000, and nobody really knew how it had happened or where the money had come from. God, it seemed, had taken charge. His house now had a kitchen, running water and mains drainage, it had been rewired and relit, it had a new belfry and a new vestry, it had been redecorated and recarpeted from end to end. No-one had set out to raise funds or appeal for money. God had paid, as he always does, for what he had ordered.

While the menfolk had been busy digging trenches, knocking holes, plumbing, wiring and painting, the womenfolk had not been idle either. There was of course the seemingly endless cleaning up. Saturday after Saturday a team moved in with extra vacuum cleaners, buckets, mops, dusters and polish, to make the place presentable for Sunday. But the Spirit of God was also moving people, as he moved Bezalel and Oholiab (Ex 31:1–11), to make beautiful things for the worship of God.

Sue had a special gift for dressmaking and needlework. She made a banner around the words from Psalm 95, 'Come let us worship and bow down'. She also made a green altar frontal with a gold dove and red flames of fire for the season of Sundays after Pentecost. Penny, who had been trained at art college, had a vision of Christ in the rising sun. She translated this into another banner which we hung over the pulpit. Sandra, who taught at the village school, made a banner with her class to illustrate, 'I am a new creation'(2 Cor 5:17). Hilda, a skilful embroiderer, made a pale green fall for the pulpit. All of a sudden, what had been a rather plain country church had come to life with colour and light. God had had his house not only modernised but beautified.

—

NINETEEN

MANY OF HIS DISCIPLES TURNED BACK

PEOPLE WERE LEAVING. In both churches people who had once been coming to church more or less regularly were no longer doing so. And this had been going on for one reason or another more or less continuously since I came.

There must be greater challenges in the world for church leaders and ministers of the gospel to face, but for most of us this is the greatest one near home. I am by nature a somewhat timid person: far from being a picker of fights, my instinct is to mollify everyone and keep them happy. But such a way of life is simply incompatible with serving God. So I have had to learn time and again to let people go. But I have never been able to do so without some anxiety and searching of my own soul. I have suffered plenty of seasons of doubt about whether what I was doing and saying was right.

At each step as the services changed at St. George's someone else left. Someone could not tolerate the children fidgeting in church, someone could not tolerate the cups of coffee being served after the service was over, someone would only come to a service at which we used the old prayer book, someone could not tolerate shaking hands with other people during the service. There was never a mass exodus, just a trickle. And God was good: as some trickled out, God sent others trickling in. Overall the size of the congregation did not seem to change much; slowly the faces changed, but the numbers did not.

In some ways the situation was more difficult at St. Nicholas'. We had taken a flourishing separate Sunday School and a flourishing monthly Family Service and amalgamated everything into a single weekly act of worship for all ages, including the children. At first this had seemed highly successful; the large Family Service congregations were being reproduced every week, and once a month when the Scouts and Guides and Brownies paraded the church would be full. But soon the cracks began to appear.

Parents who had happily sent their children to the separate Sunday School expressed resentment that they now seemed to be expected to come to church themselves. Families which had happily come to church once a month expressed resentment that they now seemed to be expected to come to church every week. We were cashing in the cheques of 'folk religion', and a good many of them bounced. Soon we found that the new Sunday School, which withdrew into the chancelroom for part of the service, had fewer children than the old Sunday School which had met separately. People wondered if we had done the right thing.

Also, the spiritual temperature in the church began to rise. One by one people were coming to a fresh conviction of faith; people were being converted and filled with the Holy Spirit. It began to show in how people talked and behaved, not only in church but out in the village. People began talking about Jesus instead of talking about the church. People you had known for years suddenly had silly smiles on their faces. In church, people were raising their hands as they sang and worshipped; they were hugging and kissing each other; there was often a sort of hush during the worship as the presence of God came down on the congregation. Often people's lives were touched deeply at such moments, but others, standing apart and resisting such changes, felt uncomfortable and angry.

People left. Some quietly faded away, others made a fuss before they went. The uniformed organisations stopped parading. One man poured out his grievances in a long and angry letter.

The services and traditions of the Church of England, of which you are a servant, have withstood the rigours of change for nearly two thousand years. Along you come, and albeit with the agreement of a minority of the congregation, decide the traditional values and services of the Church of England are no longer appropriate, and in need of change.

The act of prayer and worship for the majority is very private and sacred, not to be disturbed by a host of arm-waving, chanting sectarians. When the act of worship becomes fanatical rather than enjoyable, it is time to speak out, not as you put it 'speaking in tongues', but in plain English.

Jesus said, 'To what can I compare this generation? They are like children sitting in the market-places and calling out to others: "We played the flute for you, and you did not dance; we sang a dirge, and you did not mourn" '. (Matt 11:16–17). It seemed to be the same in our generation: if we had the old prayer book and the old chants, people said it was boring; if we had a lively service with upbeat music, people complained it was too much fun. The old traditional services never had so many friends when they were alive as they had when they were dead. A lot of people discovered they definitely preferred to stay away from the old services than from the new ones.

Then came yoga. I knew that there was a yoga class in the village, and that some of the congregation were, or had been, members of it. I knew that one or two of the congregation were quite deeply involved in yoga. I and other members of the church had spoken privately with them about this before. But then I came to a sermon which I was to preach on the baptismal promise, 'I renounce evil', and I knew that I had to give examples of the sort of practices which this meant. I also knew that there was no point in only mentioning things far away, but that I had to specify things near at home. So I tried to explain why horoscopes were wrong, and why spiritualism was wrong and why yoga was wrong.

Yoga is supposedly an alternative way of salvation. It is of course inseparably linked with Hinduism, the religion of India. It is therefore linked to the whole world of the occult and of evil spirits, of which India is so full. But even at the most superficial level, the physical exercises of yoga are offering an alternative way of salvation. No-one pretends that yoga is merely another name for aerobics or keep fit. Yoga offers peace. But it is an alternative to the peace which Jesus offers, and it is a false and deceptive peace. The Christian who has found the peace of God which passes all understanding does not need the peace of yoga, and must renounce that bogus road to peace.

It was a big stick.

One man was so angry he could hardly speak to me

as he left, and has hardly been able to speak to me since. A Sunday School teacher resigned. Altogether about half a dozen people left the church that day and some of them have never come back.

In the week before, Susan had had a revelatory dream. In her dream she had a small spot on her arm with a little black head. She squeezed the head and out came a thin black thread. She pulled the thread and as it came out it became longer and thicker. Soon she saw that it had little hooks on it and was like a worm. Someone else (Jesus) was now pulling it for her and she realised that it went right up her arm, across her chest, and had its tentacles wrapped round her heart. She cried out, 'Don't pull it out. You will pull my heart out.' But Jesus did pull it out and she felt its tentacles being torn away from her heart, setting her heart free.

This was the spirit of yoga in Sue's life. She had been to yoga classes some years before and still had yoga books in her house. On the surface it seemed such an innocent, even trivial thing—a few exercises on a mat on the floor of the village hall—but there was a sinister thread that led from there to the heart and to a grip which was difficult and painful to break. Susan renounced yoga and burned her books. But for others the grip was too strong.

People were leaving St. Nicholas', and the size of the congregation was decreasing. It was still bigger than the ordinary adult congregation used to be, but compared to the apparent initial success of our new service we seemed to be going steadily downhill. But by this time there was no turning back. The number of born-again, Spirit-filled Christians was steadily growing, and even had I contemplated turning back I knew that now the others simply would not let me. Too many people had found healing and wholeness; too many people had found love, joy and peace in the Lord to go back. Whatever the problems, whatever the disappointments, whatever the battles, there was only one way to go now—forward.

TWENTY

DO NOT FORBID
SPEAKING IN TONGUES

MATTERS CAME TO a head in the church council at St. Nicholas'. Unlike some other church councils I have known, that at St. Nicholas' did not see its mission in life as making things difficult for the rector. Indeed our meetings were always agreeable and cooperative. So it was not in a spirit of confrontation that someone raised a matter under 'Any other business'.

> About speaking in tongues, and these other things that people call out during the service. There are some people who are very uncomfortable about all this, and they don't feel that it is right in a public service. You can do those sorts of things in private company with people who understand it, and where you don't have to go if you don't want to. But not in a Sunday morning service when there are children and other people present.

God had warned me before the meeting that some sort of bomb was going to go off unexpectedly, and this was it. God had also told me to listen to what people were saying, so I did. It was too late to deal with such a matter there and then, and I guessed that this was only the tip of an iceberg, so we agreed to convene again in three weeks and really listen to what people were feeling.

What had happened over the previous two years was this: a substantial number in the congregation had cottoned on to what I had been saying. They had been baptised in the Holy Spirit. They had become hungry for more, come to midweek meetings and gone away to things like New Wine. We had learned new songs and wanted to sing them in our own church. We had got used to the things of the Spirit and believed in them. But back home on the ranch there were other people who simply came to church Sunday by Sunday and were confused and sometimes frightened by what was going on around them.

It was salutary for the eager-beavers, including me, to be made aware of all this. It was not so much opposition as a cry for help. We had to slow down or stop, at least to give others the chance to catch up, and we had to accept some pruning. We agreed on two things: first, to hold two open meetings on Sunday afternoons at which members of the congregation could express their own feelings on the one hand, and I could explain more about the gifts of the Spirit on the other and, second, the music group agreed with me to go through our repertoire of songs and hymns and prune it. We were trying to sing too many new songs for people to learn them. There was a good deal of public repentance from members of the church council, including me.

But more was being said than this. There was a minority in the congregation, spoken for by as much as speaking in the church council, who were saying not just, 'slow down' or even, 'stop', but who were saying, 'turn back'. This focused on the exercise of the gifts of the Spirit—prophecy, words of knowledge and speaking in tongues. The cries were cries of fear rather than anger. But as we were trying to look at this together, an extraordinary thing happened: Peter, a farmer on the church council, began to speak as he had never spoken before. To begin with, even I did not understand what was going on.

'Come in love not fear,' Peter said, and he repeated it four times. 'The grace of our Lord Jesus Christ—I already had this, for I am the Lord Jesus Christ. The love of God—I had already had this, because he was my Father. But even I needed the fellowship of the Holy Spirit when I was on earth. And,' Peter finished, 'we need it, now and for evermore.'

It was totally unexpected and totally without guile. Either Peter had succumbed to mad-cow-disease, or the Lord himself was trying to tell us something. We were not actually in any doubt which. I explained what I understood to be happening and explained what I understood the words to mean. Peter was prophesying: that is, Jesus himself was speaking to us through Peter. Had anyone tried to do such a thing as a stratagem it would not have worked. But after Peter had spoken, it did not seem possible to go on discussing the matter as we had been doing before, and we soon drew the meeting to a close.

In the next couple of months we held the promised open meetings and tried to deal with the fears and discontents expressed. I did my best to explain that the gifts of the Spirit were not meant to create sensations, certainly not to create fear, but to open people up to God. I did my best to reassure people that just as our earthly father will not give a child who asks for bread a stone, so God also knows how to give good gifts to his children (Matt 7:9–11). But at the end of the day I was not going to forbid speaking in tongues. In all this I had to ask myself over and over again, 'Am I right?' My correspondent in the parish had earlier accused me of altering the traditional values of the Church of England. Perhaps he was a bit short on historical perspective but certainly for a long time Church of England services had been formal, restrained and solemn. At its best such worship conveyed a powerful sense of the timelessness and serenity of God. At its more common such worship was simply tedious. Most of my correspondent's contemporaries had long since voted with their feet on traditional Church of England services of that sort. Nevertheless, what right had I, a servant of that Church, to take that tradition away from those who might still want it or might want to come back to it for old times' sake?

I had to settle with myself first the matter of whether I was primarily a servant of the Church of England or a servant of God? If a servant of God, where then did I stand in relation to the Church of England? Where, for that matter, did the Church of England stand in relation to God? What really are 'the traditional values of the Church of England'? It was in fact clear enough to me that I was a servant of God. I served him within the communion and fellowship of the Church of England and therefore I owed obedience to my bishop or overseer, and to the rules of discipline which that church had made. So far nothing I had felt obliged to do as a servant of God had brought me into conflict with either the bishop or those rules, and I sincerely hoped it would not. If such a situation arose I might in conscience have to leave the Church of England and trust God for the future. Such a resolution, I found, took away the fear of bishops! But then I did not expect such a situation to arise. I came back to the fact that the ultimate traditional value of the Church of England, as I read both its history and its documents, was the authority and sufficiency of the Scriptures. With that I could live.

It might be true that the traditions of the Church of England for a long time past had not included charismatic practices like prophecy and speaking in tongues. But Scripture explicitly says, '...be eager to prophesy and do not forbid speaking in tongues' (1 Cor 14:39). The authorised liturgies of the Church of England did not explicitly allow for such practices, but neither did they forbid them. So I concluded that I was being a faithful servant of God, and not an unfaithful servant of the Church of England, when I permitted and encouraged such things to happen in church.

When the church council of St. Nicholas' met again we reviewed the course of our discussion and I stated the position I had arrived at as the priest in charge of the parish. I enquired how many people in the Council agreed with me: sixteen did, while only two did not, and that without animosity.

It was a watershed in the life of the church. People had been heard, issues had been examined; and proper authority had been exercised. Those who disagreed did not feel rejected; those who were unhappy still felt cared for. The congregation continued to include people who were charismatic and people who were not. But something had been resolved: St. Nicholas' was a church in which the Holy Spirit was welcome and free to come and move among us, distributing his gifts as he willed, while for the sake of order and decency I was in charge of the congregation.

TWENTY ONE

THE HARVEST IS PLENTIFUL

WHEN NICODEMUS CAME to Jesus by night Jesus said to him, 'You must be born again' (Jn 3:7). He did not say to him, 'You must come to church.' Likewise, John the Baptist did not say of Jesus, 'I baptise you with water, but he will get you to come to church.' John said, 'I baptise you with water, but he will baptise you with the Holy Spirit' (Jn 1:33).

I am not in any doubt that those who are born again and baptised in the Holy Spirit should come to church. They need it, and in the ordinary course of Christian events they will do it. But there is a constant temptation, both for the church leader and for other church members, to take short cuts. Getting bottoms on seats can so easily become the name of the game. And that can so easily and devilishly become linked with getting money in the collection.

For a start, these things are much more easily measurable: we can count the number of people in church and count the amount in the offering. This is the way that business and industry counts, and we can easily adopt the same outlook. The inside of someone's relationship with God is much harder to measure. It is essentially invisible, as God is invisible. Such a relationship, despite some fairly clear landmarks, like being born again and filled with the Spirit, is also dynamic and fluid, something in movement, and therefore difficult to register and pin down.

Again, it is relatively easy to get people to come to church. It is quite possible to fill a church by putting on good entertainment: according to the social milieu, it may be lively up-beat songs, or beautiful music in the choir, or hearty *Songs of Praise*; jokes and familiarity from the pulpit, or the reinforcement of people's political prejudices, or perhaps flatteringly intellectual sermons; an associated round of coffee mornings, or dinner parties, or sausage-and-mash suppers. It is not difficult to make a church a good club. But these are all short cuts. The only thing that counts with God is changed lives, and that is something only God can do.

I needed constantly to keep my eye on the ball. I was not to be satisfied with lesser things, not even with filling the seats, certainly not with teaching people to sing new songs or perform new tricks, like raising their hands in the air. My only real satisfaction could be in seeing people born again, filled with the Spirit, healed inwardly and outwardly, and changed into the likeness of Christ. If these things were happening I need not really worry about anything else, and if they were not, it was all a waste of time anyway. But I had constantly to remind myself of this.

In fact, these things were happening; throughout everything else, sometimes in spite of everything else, lives were being changed. We had no strategy for evangelism, nor were we engaged in any particular evangelistic activities, but it was happening; God was doing it.

Chris had lost his wife a few years before, leaving him with a young son to bring up on his own. Christine had befriended him, and taken him cakes and other bits of baking from time to time. She had also taken him to hear Billy Graham, but without very much effect. Chris had had almost no Christian contacts before, neither at home as a child, nor at school, nor with a church. He was dabbling in Buddhism and spiritualism, and deeply confused. Christine also invited him to her house fellowship, where he talked a lot and learned little.

However, one Sunday morning he was in his workshop and heard the church bells ringing across the fields for the morning service. Suddenly and inexplicably he felt a desire to go to church. Changing quickly into something decent he arrived after the service had begun. Sue was introducing a worship song and saying how much Jesus loved us. Chris was overwhelmed; he found himself face to face with the greatness and the holiness and the love of God, and immediately felt unworthy and unclean. Not many minutes after he had come into church Chris left again, and went out into the churchyard and wept. Christine had noticed Chris come, and go, and she went out into the churchyard after him and helped him release all the guilt and the pain to God.

Alan (yet another Alan—I can't help it if they are all called Alan) was stuck in a traffic jam in torrential rain on the London Orbital Motorway, the M25. Alan's wife and two children all sang in the choir at St. George's, but Alan rarely came to church himself. He also had been brought up in an unbelieving family. His work involved a lot of driving to other parts of the country and on this particular day he was at a standstill on the motorway. The car radio was broadcasting a play, and the play concerned a Catholic priest. Alan was only half listening to it, but it was making him think about God and what his own attitude to God was. Suddenly he knew that he had to make a decision, that God was, as it were, actually there in the car on the M25 in the rain and asking him to say yes or no to him. Alan said yes.

Next Sunday he started coming to church. He bought a Bible and a commentary and started to read them. Some months later he was baptised (in the school swimming pool) and confirmed together with his two children. God had done it again.

Diana's life was in shreds. She had had polio as a child which had left her with a limp. She had lost her South African husband and a son, killed together in a road accident. She had become a Christian and had been befriended by a Baptist pastor before she moved to our village, but she was emotionally dependent on a friend who was positively anti-Christian. So Diana had never joined a church and her Christian life was at a standstill or even sliding back when she came to live in our village.

One Sunday morning in midsummer, she walked down to the village shop (which opened on Sunday mornings) to fetch some teabags. St. Nicholas' church is within sight of the village shop, and when she reached the shop Diana just kept on walking. She saw the church and knew she had to go in. I was halfway through my sermon when I saw her enter and sit down at the back, dressed in an old navy blue T-shirt and shorts. I was preaching a very simple sermon on the text 'God is love' (1 John 4:8), and just as Diana sat down I said, 'God loves you'. It was God who spoke those words into Diana's heart, there and then. Towards the end of the service I delivered the words of knowledge which God had given us at the Friday night prayer meeting. One word was that someone in church was crying, that God knew their trouble and wanted to comfort them. Diana was crying, and God spoke to her again. She came forward at the end of the service for personal prayer and ministry.

All three of these people became Christians in the course of a year, and there were others like them. That was not the end of the story for any of them, for Jesus said, 'Go and make disciples...' (Matt 28:19), not, 'Go and make converts.' Conversion is the beginning of the story, not the end; discipleship is a lifetime of being changed by God. But God has begun a good work in the lives of these three, and he who began this work will surely bring it to completion.

Our two churches both supported the Billy Graham Mission in 1989, and we invited people to the centre nearest to us. One man, Mike, came to St. George's as a result. Such a response multiplied right across England no doubt added up to thousands of conversions and a worthwhile reward for the prodigious expenditure of money and effort involved. But seen from our point of view Billy Graham seemed rather ineffectual. It was not that he was not an effective preacher and evangelist, nor that the Mission was not efficiently organised, but the simple fact was that at that particular moment there were not enough people in our two villages ready to be converted.

Jesus said, 'The harvest is plentiful' (Matt 9:37), and indeed it is. But in these villages harvesting people for the Kingdom of God is not so much like harvesting corn as like harvesting tomatoes. A field of corn ripens all at once, and the reaper or the combine-harvester moves into it and harvests every stalk and every ear in a single day. A crop of tomatoes, on the other hand, ripens one by one. The picker must go out day after day and gather in those which are ripe. Others are still green, others still only just beginning life as little yellow flowers. These will be the harvest next week, or the harvest in weeks to come. The joy of ministry in the local church, as opposed to the ministry of Billy Graham, is that it does not all have to happen tonight.

Perhaps God will send real revival to our villages (we do pray he will) and we will gather in great sheaves of corn all at once. For the time being the task which he has given us is that of watching and picking in the tomatoes as and when they ripen, one by one. But there is a harvest—slow perhaps, but steady—and that is exciting.

TWENTY TWO

WE KNOW IN PART

THE VILLAGE GRAPEVINE informed me that Jane had had a baby in the big hospital 50 miles away, and that the baby was very poorly—would we pray for them both? I had not met Jane at the time nor her husband David. They had been married for some years, during which Jane had worked as a hairdresser, visiting homes in the village to cut and dress people's hair. So she was widely known and well-liked. She and David had been unable to have babies in the normal way, and Laura had eventually been conceived by *in vitro* fertilization. Now Laura was fighting for her little life in an incubator.

I felt that Maureen and I should make the journey to the hospital to see Laura and her distressed parents. So on the spur of the moment that Saturday afternoon, we set off. When we arrived on the ward we introduced ourselves to David and Jane and talked with them about Laura. Laura had not breathed at birth and was still living on a ventilator. Her kidneys were not functioning and she was being fed by drips. She had convulsive movements and was being sedated. I asked permission to pray over her and anoint her with oil, which both parents and the nursing staff willingly gave. Then Maureen and I came away.

Laura did not appear to get any better, and at noon the next day the doctors told Jane and David that they were planning to switch off the ventilator. But that afternoon, to everyone's amazement, Laura started breathing by herself. Her kidneys started to function and she began to live. Three days later she was taken out of the incubator. She still had plenty of problems, and she and her mother had to stay in hospital together for several more weeks, but eventually they both came home.

It was an exciting day, and everyone recognized that a miracle had occurred. But Laura was handicapped. She grew, but as she grew it became plain that she had cerebral palsy. She had difficulty feeding. She did not have the usual control over her head or limbs. Could she see? But she went on making progress. She began to respond to sounds, and to light and shade. She smiled and laughed and responded to people. We went on praying for Laura and still do, but she has made me ask some hard questions, to which I did not and still do not have many answers.

Had God given Laura life only to leave her handicapped? Could he not have healed all her infirmities when he healed some? I do know better than to start asking whose fault it is. It is no part of the Christian healing ministry to put anyone under condemnation, including ourselves. I still believe that God wants Laura to be whole. I still believe that he can do it and I have by no means stopped hoping that he will. But I have to admit that I do not understand all his ways: he is the Sovereign Lord.

A strange sequel to Laura's story was that some two

years later Jane and David had another baby, against all medical predictions, in the normal way. Louise, thank God, was born healthy and normal.

At the other end of life, Rod and Grace were a couple of the older members of our congregation who accepted and welcomed the changes in our churches. But then Rod developed cancer. He had radiotherapy but remained weak and in pain. The doctor warned Grace that he had only a few months to live and would be gone by Christmas.

Maureen and I went to the house to pray for Rod. The Holy Spirit certainly touched him powerfully: the pain left him and over the next few weeks he recovered a lot of his health and strength. Incidentally God healed Grace at the same time, though nothing was said in prayer about her at all. She had suffered for several years with a leaky heart valve, but as we prayed for Rod she felt a great sensation of warmth round her heart, and the doctor told her later that her heart was working properly again.

Rod continued to walk with a slight limp, but he recovered so well that he was able to go back to his workshop, where he loved to make things in both wood and metal. During the summer he made a cupboard for the flower-arrangers at church. But in the autumn he began to deteriorate again. We continued to pray for him, at home and then in hospital, but just before Christmas he died.

He had lived his three-score years and ten. Especially in that last year he had lived and died, full of faith, and he and Grace knew that God had touched him. Why had God lengthened his life by just that one year? Why not more? Again questions I could ask easily enough, but could not answer. God is Sovereign.

God has continued to work signs and wonders among us, sometimes complete healings and sometimes, as with Laura and Rod, apparently only partial ones. Sometimes people get better at once, sometimes gradually. After a major heart attack which nearly took his life, Victor was healed marvellously by prayer and the laying-on of hands. After a cerebral haemorrhage which nearly took Trevor's life, he was healed by prayer and the National Health Service. Every Sunday we offer to pray for those who are sick, and minister to them at the end of the service. God continues to heal, but never so that we can take it for granted. We have learnt to expect God to act and to rely on him to bless, but not so that we can ever presume on what he will do or how he will do it. We have learnt to say simply, as we begin to pray over people, 'Let's see what God will do.'

Oddly enough our biggest problem with the healing ministry has been to persuade people to use it. In the two parishes we now have a healing ministry team of nearly thirty people. But that means that most of the time we have many more people willing to pray than people willing to be prayed for. More prayer ministry takes place in homes, in the street, and, yes, over the counter of the electrical shop, though now the current is usually passing the other way. But the fact remains that it requires faith, not only to lay hands on the sick in Jesus' name and expect them to recover, but to receive the laying-on of those hands. A lot of people in this generation, even among the churched as well as among the unchurched, simply do not have enough faith to come forward.

We read in the gospels of all those who came to Jesus for healing. There were a great many of them. They came with every sort of ailment, every disease and infirmity of body, mind and spirit. And Jesus healed them all (e.g. Matt 4:23–24). Likewise, the Apostles after him (Acts 5:12–16). 'Jesus Christ is the same yesterday and today and for ever (Heb 13:8). Therefore I believe that Jesus wills that all should be healed, and pray over the sick with that expectation. I have grown from being surprised when people are healed to being surprised when they are not. But sometimes they are not, and we have all had to face the questions that then arise. I know all the stock answers, and I also know that in the end I don't know. But one thing I have learned: that no one has ever been hurt by our praying for them. I have not known anyone whose faith was damaged even when no physical healing ensued. When we have prayed over the sick, every one has been blessed, many physically, all spiritually. So we go on doing it.

TWENTY THREE

YOU ARE THE BODY
OF CHRIST

WHEN MAUREEN AND I first moved to these new parishes, Christmas was only weeks away. Even before my licensing I had had meetings with both sets of churchwardens and had asked, 'What do you do at Christmas? What is going to happen?' I simply took over the existing arrangements. At St. Nicholas' this meeting with the churchwardens became a regular monthly fixture. As our wives were as committed and involved in the life of the church as we were it seemed natural to include them in our discussions, and soon the six of us had a regular engagement to eat together and discuss what was going on.

For the first year it was mostly a matter of me saying, 'What do you do in Lent, at Easter, on Gift Day, at Harvest Festival, on Remembrance Sunday, for the Sunday School anniversary (or whatever event was coming up)?' Such discussions soon broadened out from questions of what we did to questions of what we ought to do. I believed in sharing leadership, in any case, and here I found an opportunity to do so with four of the people in the parish who already held positions of responsibility and were exercising some sort of leadership in the church. It was only an informal arrangement—decisions which meant changes in the life of the church had to be taken in the parochial church council—but this was an opportunity to talk things over which I found increasingly valuable and important.

At St. George's there was a different relationship between the rector and the congregation. The church council had actually asked the bishop for 'a leader'. There was a more distinct sense of hierarchy, and an obvious hankering after a more traditional style of clerical leadership. The idea (and in fact the memory) of the rector as the father of the village—benevolent, generous and autocratic—still exercised a romantic attraction at St. George's. Never mind that I did not any longer live in the gracious and spacious Georgian rectory, nor that, for that matter, I did not live in the village at all. Never mind that most of the villagers did not want a father figure, and would have strongly resented that sort of interference in their lives. The myth lived on.

Unfortunately, the consequence of this sort of relationship had always been a stifling of any sort of Christian leadership in the parishioners themselves. It was partly a social pattern, and partly an over-emphasis on the Scriptural image of the sheep and the shepherd. The shepherd's job is to do the leading; the sheep's job is simply to follow, with more or less bleating. Once people have been taught to identify themselves as sheep, it is difficult to stop them behaving like it. That does not mean that they become docile and willing followers. It simply means a reluctance to leave the herd and share in the more lonely and exposed task of leading the flock.

Of course, the reluctance to share leadership has

historically not been all on one side. The clergy themselves have often been zealous in preserving their proprietary rights. Lay officers of the Church of England, churchwardens and members of church councils, have been expected to concern themselves with the fabric and finances of the church, not with spiritual leadership. That has been jealously guarded as the prerogative of the clergyman alone.

Such an arrangement might have worked, after a fashion, in the days when every church had its own vicar. But today in the English countryside, several churches, even as many as ten or twelve, may have to share one parson. The result is simply that many parish churches, including St. George's, now have no resident leadership at all. People think of country churches as railway coaches, each with its handful of passengers and waiting to be hitched up to some clergyman like an engine before they can go anywhere. Scripture portrays churches more as motor coaches, each with its own engine and other functions built in. Scripture, admittedly, does not mention engines at all, but it does compare the church to a body, and each body has its own complete set of limbs and organs. Most Anglican churches in rural areas today have a lot of vital parts missing.

It is quite clear that these parts are not going to be supplied again in any foreseeable future by more clergymen of the traditional sort. The leadership which churches need will have to come from some other source. It may be that God will raise up leaders from within the churches themselves. In a healthy, growing church this is what will happen. But the fact is that many of the old churches and chapels in the countryside are far from vigorous and healthy: not a few look terminally ill. Leadership is quite simply the biggest problem in country churches today.

After two years at St. Nicholas' we faced a change in the churchwardenship since John decided to stand down in favour of someone younger. It was time to open up the question of shared leadership and to formalise, one way or another, the very fruitful meetings that the churchwardens and I and our wives had been having. We discussed in the church council and with the bishop the possibility of creating an eldership. Local church leaders in the New Testament are called elders, and perhaps an eldership chosen from among the local Christians was what we needed. In many ways it seemed that it would be a natural development of what we had. But we found ourselves stumbling over the name, and underneath that, stumbling over a deeper unresolved issue.

An eldership in fact introduces confusion into an Anglican church. The ordained ministers of the Church of England are already officially called presbyters or elders. As an eldership the existing ordained ministry is gravely defective: whereas in the New Testament there were several elders in every church, in the present-day Church of England there are often several churches to every elder. But the vestiges of an eldership do already exist, and to introduce or superimpose another one is only to breed confusion.

The deeper issue, not often addressed at all in the Church of England, is that of authority. The elders are those in authority in the local church. This was the point at which our church council at St. Nicholas' instinctively jibbed. It was not a reluctance to accept responsibility on anyone's part, but a perception that the establishment of an authoritative eldership was not, at that stage, what we were trying to do.

What we set up in the end was simply a steering committee for the church council, consisting of myself, the churchwardens and four elected members. What we were looking for was not so much an authoritative group as a prophetic one: a group who would try to discern with me God's leading and guidance for the life of our church, to hear what the Spirit was saying. It left the structure of authority in the church unaltered. This was a time of groping in the thicket of inherited structures and institutions for a more effective and more Scriptural pattern of leadership.

One of the frequent confusions in all the churches is between authority and ministry. Many of the ministries of our two churches were already being shared: in both churches we already had teams of people who read the Bible in church, said the prayers, taught the children and young people, led the house fellowships and shared in the healing ministry. The only two ministries which I could not share were those of preaching (which requires the bishop's licence) and celebrating the sacraments (which requires ordination). However, I was no less anxious that these also should be shared and that each church should be equipped with its own properly authorised and local ministers of the word and sacraments.

I preached and spoke about this on one or two occasions and some months later Alan, one of the churchwardens at St. Nicholas', offered himself for ordination as a non-stipendiary minister. After the usual lengthy process of selection and testing, Alan was accepted by the bishop as a candidate for ordination, and began a three-year part-time course of training and preparation. He is still the headmaster of the village school. He is not going away to be a vicar in some other part of the country. He will be ordained here to share with me the ministry of word and sacrament. He will then also share with me in the particular ministry of exercising authority in the local church, for he will be a fellow elder.

We need more such 'elders', several, it seems to me, in each parish. I understand from the Scriptures that Jesus gives to each local church the ministries and the ministers that it needs (Eph 4:11–12). It is a long and slow process by which an embryo grows into a mature human body: a single cell multiplies and gradually limbs and organs become differentiated and develop, until they are able to fulfil their specialised functions. The building up of the body of Christ is a similar process.

—

TWENTY FOUR

LOVE ONE ANOTHER

S O MANY HURTING people! The world is a battle-field. Sometimes it is open warfare with guns and tanks and bombs. We are not surprised then when there are casualties and devastation. The rest of the time we have an illusion of peace, but there is no peace. People are always hurting and being hurt.

Every new person who comes to church and every new Christian is another new arrival in the casualty ward. Some have only minor wounds, a few cuts and bruises, some are walking wounded, while others are stretcher cases, some with horrific injuries. I once had a mental picture of the church as a hospital: instead of the pews there were beds all round the walls. Some of the patients were up and about, helping the other patients. There were some people with qualifications in medicine and nursing, but they were also patients themselves. There was only one whole person among them, and that was Jesus, who was going from bed to bed healing and restoring. But it was slow work. There was so much to put right in all the patients and Jesus could only deal with a bit at a time. The patients were all recovering, some of them were getting quite fit and strong, there was an atmosphere of cheerfulness and hope—but it was a casualty ward.

The true picture is obscured because most of the people who come to church are pretending that they are perfectly well. To carry on with our daily lives we fix ourselves up with various crutches and braces, we cover up our wounds, and in some cases we are not even aware that we have quite serious injuries. But they are there all the same, impairing our performance and spoiling our enjoyment of the life God has given us.

Vera had had a close relationship with her father, but she had also been excessively protected. When other children had been riding round on bikes, Vera had been forbidden to have one, in case she hurt herself on it. Without realising it, she absorbed this spirit of anxiety about herself and the threats which the world held for her, and when she grew up she found herself to be nervous of public places and new situations and subject to attacks of panic.

When she was twenty-six her father died in a horrible accident: he spilled a garden weedkiller on to an open cut and without realising it absorbed the poison into his body. He had an agonising and sudden death. Vera experienced all sorts of conflicting emotions: resentment that she had not been able to say goodbye, anger at a God who could 'do such a thing' to her father, and fear. Her fears increased as the years went on. She could not enter a restaurant or café, or eat and drink in the company of others; she needed to sit near the door in church so that, if necessary, she could make a quick exit. She also had a particular fear of being out in her own garden and of noisy radios. She had lived at one time next door to some unpleasant neighbours who had persecuted them through the party wall with aggressive rock music.

Vera and her husband Brian moved into one of our villages and started to come to church, sitting (of course) right at the back. They had been used to a traditional country parish church, and were surprised by some of the things that they found at St. Nicholas'. They were surprised by the warmth which surrounded them from the first time they came, and they were surprised by the ministry of healing. Vera, however, came forward after a few weeks for prayer. Members of our healing ministry team prayed with her on one or two occasions, but also suggested that she should come to Maureen and me for more help.

So once a week for several weeks Vera came to talk. I would hesitate to call this 'counselling' because neither Maureen nor I have any more than minimal training or experience as counsellors. But Vera talked about her problems and we helped her to discover the roots of them. There were three things we found we had to do. The first was to correct Vera's idea of God. He was not a capricious and sadistic dictator who, at a whim, had inflicted a horrible fate on the father she loved, and might at any moment do the same again, to her or to someone else she loved and depended upon. Such things happened, in some way, because the world was a fallen world and in the power of the evil one. The evil one was her enemy; God was her friend. God has sent Jesus to rescue us from such a world and put things right. He could take care of her father, and would take care of her if she trusted him to do so.

The second thing we had to help Vera to do was to let go of her father. She was still clinging on to her memory of him and to all the emotions surrounding his death, because they were all that she had of him to cling on to and because he had been her protection. So she had to release her father to God. But before she was able to do that, she had to find another Father in God. So we lent her a Christian music tape which contained a song with the following words.

> 'Father, I can call you Father,
> For I am your child,
> Today, tomorrow and always.
> You are my Father.'
> (Danny Daniels © Mercy Publishing)

We taught her when she prayed to say, 'Father'. We also gave her a text from the Bible written out on a postcard to keep in her handbag.

> 'I will be with you; I will never leave you
> nor forsake you...Be strong and courageous.
> Do not be terrified; do not be discouraged,
> for the Lord your God will be with you wherever
> you go' (Josh 1:5,9).

We prayed with her each time she came to talk. We invited her to commit her life afresh to Jesus and to be filled with the Holy Spirit, which she did. We asked the Holy Spirit to come and heal her and help her. She cried a good deal at these times, but she changed. She increased in confidence. She started eating and drinking in public, and went out to restaurants. She took her coffee out and sat in the garden. Some nervousness remained, and she had to continue to work at her healing. But it was real.

A great deal has been written about 'inner healing'. It is certainly true that a great many of our hurts lie inside and not outside us. These in particular are not wounds which are to be healed lightly. It is usually necessary for the wounds to be opened up for the infection to be expelled, and that is often a painful and distressing process. But, when all is said and done, I believe that the process of healing is usually quite simple. One of three medicines seem to treat most of these illnesses: a right understanding of the fatherhood of God; the knowledge of the forgiveness of sins through the blood of Jesus; and the release of forgiveness and goodwill towards those who have sinned against us.

Yet one more medicine is the most important of all, which needs to be mixed with all the others: love itself. It is said that the apostle John in his old age simply kept repeating one simple message, 'Love one another'. That is what people need more than anything else: all-forgiving, all-embracing, unending love. It is the love of God, but we can be such powerful agents of this love of God to one another. It was within the loving fellowship of the church that Vera felt able to ask for prayer and help. It was within the love of our sitting room that Vera felt able to reveal her hurts. It is love that heals.

Without love, all our speaking in tongues is just a discordant noise. Without love, all our prophetic visions and words of knowledge are not worth anything. The ultimate value in the kingdom of God is the quality of our life together—the warmth, the genuineness, the endurance of our love for one another.

—

TWENTY FIVE

YOU CANNOT SERVE GOD AND MAMMON

MOST ENGLISH COUNTRY churches are locked into a nightmare about money. Medieval buildings demand constant, sometimes major, repair just to keep them standing up. The diocese clamours for more and more money with which to pay the clergy. Nevertheless, the number of paid clergy continues to decline and the number of people in the village supporting the church and paying the bills also gets smaller year by year.

The church in the countryside has often become not much more than a self-perpetuating, fund-raising organisation, the sole purpose of whose existence seems to be to raise funds to go on existing to raise funds...nothing more soul-destroying and dispiriting can be imagined. Any vestigial flicker of enthusiasm or energy for the real mission of the church is snuffed out by the demands for money, and many country churches have lost all hope or even idea of this ever changing. Many a rural church council sees itself only as a committee for planning the next fête or bazaar, and not a few people are quite happy to have it so.

It is a long historical road which has led the country parish to this point, and it is not easy to break the spiritual stranglehold which Mammon has established. The countryman, even the Christian countryman, has never in history really had to give. In the Middle Ages, the church itself was probably built by the lord of the manor and some land, the glebe, was allocated to the parish priest for his support. The Church of England became a wealthy institution through such endowments, and we still have the dubious benefits of that historic wealth in the hands of the Church Commissioners. But, meanwhile, the ordinary man in the village pew never learnt that it was part of his Christian profession to give money to God.

Christians in all the other churches, not least in the new house churches, have always understood that without such giving the church would not be able to function, but this simple fact of life has been obscured for members of the Church of England. Many other Christians take the practice of tithing for granted, but that is a particularly emotive word in a country parish.

In the Middle Ages, the tithe was a church tax that was legally levied on all those who farmed the land, whether willing or unwilling. Although commuted in various ways over the years, the final vestiges of this legal tithe only disappeared in 1977. Well into living memory the tithe in the countryside was a legally enforceable and much resented tax.

The fact remains that a tenth of our income is the standard which, both by teaching and example, the Scriptures set before us as what God expects his people to give. To this standard of giving God has attached wonderful promises of his own provision (Mal 3:6–12). No minister of the word committed to sharing with his people the whole counsel of God can do his duty and omit to present them both with this challenge and with these promises. Indeed, the Church of England is in the mess it is financially simply because it has ignored and still largely ignores this word of God.

For the first six months in these parishes I ignored the subject of money altogether; there were many other things which came first. But I knew that I would have to talk about money eventually and I knew that it would not get any easier for being put off. So in our first summer I invited the members of the two church councils to spend a Saturday away together to think about the subject of Christian giving. I told them of my own experience for four years of 'living by faith', living without an assured income at all and relying on God to provide. I then laid the challenge before everyone of exercising the same faith in God to provide for us if we took him at his word and gave him a tenth of all we got.

For a year we left it at that and then the following summer invited every member of each congregation to a special supper at which I gave notice that I would speak about the giving of money to God. Before these meetings I experienced the same sort of trepidation that I had often experienced earlier: the knowledge that what I had to say could, and probably would, cause offence. But I had long since learnt to recognise such trepidation as a spiritual barrier which had to be broken: it was the devil defying me to attack his strongholds. Attack them I must.

The love of money is a root of much evil (1 Tim 6:10). That is why Jesus spoke so much about money himself. It has often been said that when a person is baptised the last part to get wet is his wallet. Teaching Christians everywhere how to master Mammon and to conquer the love of money is a major challenge.

Every year now I make one special occasion to

preach the gospel of tithing. Every year now it gets easier. Every year more people respond. We have never set out to register or measure people's response. We have never asked anyone to make an overt financial commitment. But steadily the income of the two parishes has gone up. Each year there is a certain amount of squawking as Mammon feels the point of the sword, but there is an acceptance growing in the churches that tithing is the supernatural Christian thing to do. More than that, there is a cheerfulness about the giving that never existed before.

Stuart and Brenda heard the message one year about giving a tenth, and went home and studied Malachi 3. Stuart was an engineer in a local food-processing factory. He had a mortgage and two children under five. But he and Brenda reckoned that to give God a tenth of their income and to have the floodgates of heaven opened for them sounded like a good deal. So they decided to take God at his word, and do as he invited them to do and put him to the test.

All went well; they started to tithe and were never short of anything they needed. They found, as everybody who has ever done this has found, that ninety per cent in God's economy goes as far as one hundred per cent in the world's. Then the bomb fell: Stuart was made redundant. It was happening to lots of people at the time and Stuart and Brenda felt no particular resentment about it. The same thing had happened to Stuart some years before.

At that time Stuart had not been a Christian, and the whole experience of being out of work had been a traumatic and agonising one for both Brenda and him. They had been worried about money, about finding another job; they had become edgy with each other and restless. This time round they had Jesus with them. There was no anxiety, no impatience, just a simple trust and peace in their hearts. But they had to reconsider their tithing. Stuart went on to the dole and his income dropped to a third of what it had been before. Would they be able to manage at all, let alone continue to give a tenth to God?

They decided in fact that they needed God to open the floodgates of heaven even more now than they had done before, so they resolved to continue to take God at his word and give him their tithe. They have testified publicly at one of our services that they wanted for nothing. They experienced no anxiety about money. They never really knew just how it all happened, but whenever the bills came in there was enough money to pay for them. They proved the faithfulness of God.

In the end I have discovered that that is the main purpose of the practice of tithing: to prove the faithfulness of God. It is indeed the God-given way of providing for the needs of the church and its full-time ministers. But even more importantly, it is the God-given way of proving for ourselves God's care and provision. The poorer a person is the more blessed they will be by tithing. We learn in this simple and practical way to trust God to look after us, to rely on him and not on ourselves, to put him first and to believe his word.

It becomes a sweet addiction. Those who have learned the joy of giving always seem to want to give more. We are led on to exceed the righteousness of the scribes and Pharisees who tithed, and give more than a tenth. To be set free to give is part of the glorious liberty of the children of God.

—

TWENTY SIX

REMEMBER THE POOR

EVERY YEAR I go away for a retreat. It is usually just before Advent begins, at the end of November—three or four days spent in complete silence with the Lord. Since we moved to St. George's and St. Nicholas' at the same time of the year, my annual retreat has been also an anniversary of our move, and it has been an opportunity to look back and give thanks for what God has done and also to stand back and look with God at where we are. So three years after first coming to these two churches I packed my bag as usual and went off to a nearby convent to stay in silence with the nuns.

During this particular time of relaxation and prayer it seemed to me that God was saying that we must remember the poor. I was of course well aware that during these past three years our concentration had been very largely focused on ourselves, on our own relationship with God, on our own worship, on our own health and wholeness (both physical and spiritual), on our own relationships with each other, and on our own church buildings and finances. I was also aware of how easily a church can simply become absorbed in its own affairs and forget the world outside which Christ came to save, and not least how easily a charismatic church can become a 'bless-me' club. But it is not possible for finite human beings to do everything at once. The attempt to do too many things, too quickly, with too few resources tends to mean that little is actually achieved; people become discouraged because the burdens on their time and energy are too great, and nothing is done properly. I was aware all along that we had to do things in God's time and order. But now it seemed that on God's agenda it was time for us to remember the poor.

But there are an awful lot of poor and needy people in the world, with a lot of different sorts of poverty and need. We first had to discover which poor and needy people God had in mind for us to help. There is a certain paralysis which comes over us when we contemplate the needs of the world: we feel like the disciples, faced with five thousand people to feed and only five small loaves, 'What are these among so many?' (Jn 6:9). It is easy to despair of being able to do anything significant before the ocean of the world's needs. Where do we start? Whose need do we try to meet?

We prayed about these questions in the church council at St. Nicholas', and then we each wrote down any special need of which we were aware which God seemed to be laying on our hearts. After the meeting we analysed the responses, and identified five areas of need which God seemed to be pointing out: the spiritual need of the gospel both at home and abroad, the physical needs of people in the Third World and in countries of Eastern Europe, the needs of men in our local prison, the needs of the unemployed in our own village, and the needs of the homeless in our own country. A spate of funerals at about this time also brought home to me the needs of widows and widowers in our own communities, which have a high proportion of retired people.

All of this still left us a wide enough field to get lost, and we had to wait on God to show us more specific steps and projects to undertake. First, I received a circular letter from Stephen, a professional employment counsellor and a Christian, who was offering a free service to the unemployed called 'Action Workwise'. Stephen lived just a few miles away in a neighbouring village and was open to coming over and starting a programme in our village for the unemployed. We already had the ideal venue in the village, a 'Call-In' by the village green which was used by many organizations for small group activities. So once a fortnight we hired the Call-In and opened the door for anyone in the village facing redundancy or living with unemployment to come in and share their troubles and receive Stephen's professional help.

Some of the early visitors were members of our own church. Roger, the bell-ringer, had recently been made redundant by his firm. He had been a radio officer on merchant ships crossing the English Channel and had often been away from home for weeks at a time. But now he felt discarded and useless. He was depressed about the prospects of finding work and could only see a future of enforced inactivity at home. Stephen gave Roger back some measure of hope and self-esteem. It was the job that was redundant, he explained, not Roger. Roger started to believe in himself again and seriously tackled the task of finding a job. Six weeks after we had first opened at the Call-In Roger called at the rectory one morning with good news. He was back in work! Another shipping company, at Felixstowe, had taken him on and he was due to start in a few days time.

Not everyone who came for help was to meet with such immediate success, but the counselling and support goes on, touching people at a point of real need.

Meanwhile, I had received another letter from a nearby house church leader inviting me and other members of our congregation to a seminar about ministry to the widowed. I went and took Grace. Grace's husband, Rod, had died of cancer some six months before and Grace was just beginning to find her own feet again and to make a new life for herself on her own. She and I were riveted by the speaker, who shared with us God's special love and compassion for widows, and described for us with great insight their needs. Grace and I came home determined to reach out in a new way to the widowed in our own community.

We compiled a list of those known to us who had lost a partner in the last couple of years, especially those who seemed to be struggling on their own. Grace went round and visited them all, sharing her own recent experience and listening to their grief, often for hours at a time. Her visits alone released many pent up emotions and tears, but she also invited them to come to a mutual support group, to be called 'New Beginnings'. 'New Beginnings' began its monthly meetings with eight widows and one widower and grew from there.

A third time I received a letter in the post, this time from a group of Christians in the neighbouring market town who were organising a relief convoy to take aid into Romania. On previous visits they had established contacts with Christians and churches, orphanages and aid agencies in the region of Bacau, and now they were returning with a shopping list of desperately needed items. We invited them over to St. Nicholas' to tell us all about their project and to show slides of the country and the people. Harrowing pictures of neglected orphans, echoing the ones on our television screens, moved many to tears.

Our two churches committed themselves to providing 600 children's toothbrushes, 600 tubes of children's toothpaste, and 600 combs. In addition we collected blankets, nappies, underclothes, socks, colouring books, crayons, packets of biscuits and sweets. Other churches in the area collected other items, and the team took many Bibles and other items of Christian literature to distribute through the churches.

God had opened our hearts and minds and laid upon them some of the needs of his lost and fallen world. Then he had shown us, one by one, practical ways to help.

TWENTY SEVEN

—

COME OVER INTO MACEDONIA

'THE LORD GAVE and the Lord has taken away; may the name of the Lord be praised' (Job 1:21).

When we started to sing the new songs at St. Nicholas' the Lord gave us Becky, Carol and Karen. Two years later he took them all away. Becky went away to college, and although she continued to grow in the Christian life she was no longer available to play in our music group. Carol's husband Al was posted to the US Air Force in Spain and Al, Carol and little Lucy all left our village to our great loss. Karen and her husband James also moved away from our area, and in just a few months we found ourselves nearly back where we started.

However, as fast as the Lord took away he also gave again. Just before Becky went away to college Heather started coming to church. She had lived in the village for a couple of years but had never been to church before. Heather was a music teacher! Heather gave her life to the Lord, and when Becky left Heather took over at the piano. When Carol and Karen also left, Heather moved over and played the guitar, and Sandra began to play the piano. Occasionally Heather would put down the guitar and take up her first instrument, her clarinet, which she played exquisitely.

So the worship continued, and continued to develop and grow. We had already moved away from the traditional habit of using hymns or songs as a sandwich where each hymn was sandwiched between two other parts of the service. We now had a more extended time of praise and worship at the beginning of the service with, perhaps, a hymn and three or four songs sung more or less continuously. This is an entirely different way of worshipping God from following a traditional order of service. Learning to participate in worship is always like learning to swim. I remember sinking without trace in my youth when first confronted with a service from the Anglican *Book of Common Prayer*. Now here was a new way of worshipping which leaders, musicians and congregation alike had to learn again from scratch.

Looking back I am amazed at the patience and forbearance that the congregation showed. We often stumbled and experienced those moments of human despair when we faced the contrast between the glory of God and the painful inadequacy of our own efforts to praise him. But even that is a sort of worship.

Worship is not just singing hymns or songs; in fact, singing hymns and songs is not necessarily worship at all. Worship depends on achieving some awareness of the presence and the perfection of God. There are all sorts of ways of achieving this: silence can be one of the most effective, but difficult to achieve with a church full of children. Music is another. It is not primarily an exercise of the mind; it belongs more to the heart and the spirit. The words are important, but so is the music itself. Most people need time to engage with God. The church down the ages has known the spiritual value of repetition. Worship really begins when we cease to be occupied with either the words or the music and are aware only of God. And in the end that is a grace which God alone can give: we can do our bit to draw near to God, but we depend on him to draw near to us, if our worship is not to be a formality.

Even doing our bit needs skill and practice, both on the part of the musicians and the worship leader and on the part of the congregation. Our worship did get better as time went on. We were able to be aware more of God and less of the mechanics of singing. We learnt in particular that worship was deeper if virtually nothing was said and we simply moved from song to song. But after about three years we had reached a point where our worship could not progress any further because of our musical limitations. God was blessing us; everyone was doing their best, but there was a hunger to enter into the Holy of Holies which was often frustrated as, musically speaking, we tripped over the threshold.

One day I prayed about this problem and I was reminded again of someone whom I had known, slightly, a few years before. Tony was a first-class musician and also a born-again, Spirit-filled Christian. At the time that I had known him previously his musical gift was not being used in his own church. I did not know what had become of him since then; indeed, I thought he might even have gone abroad, but I felt that I should try to get in touch again. It seemed a preposterous and presumptuous thing to suggest, but might he feel that God was calling him to 'come over to Macedonia and help us' (Acts 16:9)?

Miraculously, three months later Tony was committed to moving house and moving his piano-teaching practice in order to come and train our music group, lead our worship, and join our fellowship. From the time Tony came our worship was set free from many of its former frustrations and we experienced a new freedom in entering into the presence of God.

Tony is a particular example of the way in which many churches—especially village churches but perhaps other churches too—may need to import resources of leadership. It is mostly taken for granted that churches will receive a trained pastor from outside the congregation and outside the local community. A large town or suburban church may also advertise for an organist. But apart from that, little thought is given by anyone to moving people with leadership gifts into the places where they are needed.

In the Church of England especially and in other older denominations this may be a more fruitful model of 'church planting' than some of the other ones currently on offer. In the countryside particularly, our problem is not too few churches, but too few people and too few leaders in the churches we already have. The job of planting a church in every village and every hamlet was completed here a thousand years ago. The challenge now is to revive those churches. I believe that that will involve the transplanting of leadership resources in a new way.

It is not an easy operation, especially in a village context. As with any transplant there is an acute danger of rejection. Villagers are notoriously suspicious of outsiders, and although in many places greater social mobility has broken down the more extreme forms of parochialism, it still requires a great deal of tact and patience to come into a village and take any sort of leading role in its life.

There has to be an initial sense of need in the body if a transplant is to be acceptable. A church, like a person, that recognises itself to be ill, even terminally ill, is in a position to consider a transplant. If a vital organ has stopped functioning or been removed the body may welcome a new one. Even then the process of finding the right replacement, of matching the tissue so to speak, is not easy.

There is also trauma for the donating body. There must be a church elsewhere that is willing to give up one or more of its members, to bless them and send them out like missionaries. This itself goes against the grain for many churches, even strong ones. Too often lively churches act like sponges, sucking in people and talents from other churches round about, maybe over quite a wide area, rather than sending out their best and brightest to be the seeds of new life elsewhere. Britain is a mission field again, and churches ought to be as eager to send out missionaries into the darker places of our own land as Victorian churches were to send out missionaries to Africa.

Then there is also trauma for those who go. If leadership is to be transplanted into a village church the leader will have to move into the village. It is impossible to lead from outside. This is true even for the existing clergy. I am responsible for both St. Nicholas' and St. George's churches. I happen to live in the parish of St. Nicholas'. I certainly cannot live in both villages at once. The greatest need of St. George's church is leadership resident in the village.

For the most part we are not talking about full-time, paid leaders. At present, and for some time to come, most village churches are not going to be able to afford more paid leaders than they already have. We are talking about tent-makers: people who can move to where they are needed and not just live but work there alongside the other members of the local church and community. It may be a lonely life in spiritual terms— being a missionary always was. A sympathetic and imaginative ministry of oversight is vital to the success of the whole operation. But I believe that this is the only way forward for large areas of our countryside.

We worked through all these questions in the process of transplanting Tony to be our worship leader. If the operation was successful, as it was, it was more through the grace of God and the grace of the congregation, particularly that of the music group at St. Nicholas', than through my own expertise in handling it. In the process I gained valuable insights into both how and how not to do it. God in his mercy was ultimately in charge. Transplants are not easy for anyone, not for the receiving church or the donating church, or for the transplants themselves. But with the help of God they can be done. I look forward to the day when St. Nicholas' and St. George's can give as well as receive, for that is more blessed still.

TWENTY EIGHT

—

THE LEADERS TOOK
THE LEAD

DURING MY FOURTH Christmas in these parishes
the heating system at St. George's broke down!
This time it was not a question of freezing up,
but that the old boiler had simply worn out and burst.
But the result was the same: no heating, and no money
immediately available to pay for a new boiler. It was
clear that we faced a long winter in a cold church.
Round the corner, however, was the new church school,
which we had the right to use on Sundays and which
had a bright, warm hall. So I suggested that for the
duration of the winter we move into the school. A
majority of the congregation, especially the elderly and
those with small children, favoured the idea, but the
choir and organist were solidly against it. Eventually
the matter was decided in the church council, and the
main morning service at 9.30 a.m. moved into the
school.

The choir and the organist, however, refused to
come, so we had to improvise the music. Linda could
play the piano, very well as it turned out. Irene played
the recorder, also very expertly. So off we went.
Another week, and Susie announced that she also could
play the recorder. Why not form a music group, with a

few singers as well? The music group began to practice together and to learn new songs. We discovered that modern songs lent themselves much better to this sort of a group than to the organ and choir, and the service acquired a much greater variety of music than it ever had before. As well as enjoying the new music, the congregation found a new togetherness in the less formal and more intimate atmosphere of the primary school hall.

There we stayed for nearly three months. During that time individual members of the choir changed their minds and joined us, to everyone's relief. But as Easter approached we knew that, like some orbiting spacecraft, we had to prepare for the tricky moment of re-entry. The tricky bit was that now we had two separate sources of music: the organist and robed choir on the one hand, and the new music group on the other. There was no question in my mind of disbanding the latter or of returning to the old status quo. I reckoned that we had moved forward in the school; we might move back into the church building but we were not simply going to go back to the old ways. But could we avoid the two groups being not just separate, but rivals? Could we avoid having the choir in the blue corner and the music group in the red corner? When the bell rang for the service they might come out fighting.

Everyone saw the danger, and no-one wanted it to be like that. So our return to church at Easter time was marked by an extraordinary upsurge of goodwill on both sides, and the choir and the music group met, literally, with embraces in the middle. A joint practice was established, and everyone made an effort to mend broken fences and work together.

One of those who had moved forward most in the school was Susie. The very first Sunday we were in the hall we had ended the service with the song, 'Shine, Jesus, Shine'. I could not help noticing that Susie was singing with her eyes full of tears and both her arms stretched out towards God. This was not the old Susie. A young mother of three, she was not given to that sort of thing. God had come into her life two or three times in the past, but not, it seemed, in a very permanent way. She had started coming to church two years before, more for the sake of the children than herself. She was wary of people who waved their arms, and highly sceptical of the idea of healing and speaking in tongues.

A few weeks later Maureen had coffee one morning with Susie, and Susie talked about many things that had happened in her life. As I called to fetch Maureen about midday I was told, 'Susie wants us to pray for her. She has two lumps, in her abdomen and under her arm. She has to see a specialist about them tomorrow.' So we sat, three in a row on the sofa, and prayed that Jesus would take those lumps away. If Susie had been standing up she would have fallen down, because when we got up to go she could hardly stand upright. She leant weakly against a wall as she said goodbye to us at the door, the power of God resting upon her was so strong and so heavy. God healed Susie. The lumps had disappeared when she went to see the specialist next day. More than that, God cured Susie of her scepticism. She did not doubt the awesome power of God after that.

After Easter Linda and Susie asked Maureen if she would start meeting with them and help them to form a fellowship for young mothers like themselves. Five of them started meeting with Maureen once a week, eager to find out more about the Holy Spirit. On the second occasion Susie asked to be baptised in the Spirit and Maureen prayed and laid hands on her. The others held back at that point but Linda begged a lift home in the car with Maureen. Linda lived out in an isolated shepherd's cottage, and driving down the dark lanes she asked Maureen to stop and pray for her too.

Next day Susie was on the rectory doorstep hardly able to contain her excitement. 'Guess what!' she exclaimed. 'You'll never believe this—I've started speaking in tongues. It went on for about half an hour. I just can't believe it. I did not believe it was real.' Linda, with her own secret to share, took her sandwiches up to Susie's for lunch. She told Susie how she had chickened out of asking for the baptism of the Spirit at the meeting but had asked Maureen to pray for her privately in the car. 'You rat,' said Susie. Susie then went on to tell Linda how she had started speaking in tongues. 'You rat,' said Linda.

Next week the other three were baptised in the Spirit as well.

One person at St. George's found the new musical regime impossible to accept—the organist. A lifelong Anglo-Catholic, used, until his retirement, to an impeccable performance of the liturgy in a city church, he found the combination of our more homespun worship, modern music and charismatic Christianity deeply distasteful, even offensive. He had stayed with us as long as he had only out of a sense of duty, to support his parish church, to improve our musical standards, and to stick up for what he believed to be the catholic faith and practice of the Church of England. But four months after we came back into the church building he finally resigned as organist, at least at the morning service.

It was in the end the best solution for all of us. In the nature of the case the leader or leaders of a church are the ones who must do the leading. Other members must in the end either follow or leave. It is a dilemma which many Christians have faced, finding themselves in a church with whose leader they have disagreed. It is a dilemma which often faces charismatics in non-charismatic churches, and it can arise just as well the other way round. In such circumstances it may be praiseworthy to stay to support the leadership, in the hope of change for the better. But it is no help to anyone simply to stay to fight.

The problem is particularly difficult in a village. In a town of any size there will be a variety of churches. Most people will attach themselves to a church where they feel more or less at home and where they are not in unbearable tension with the leadership. In a village that choice probably does not exist. In a minority of villages there will be a chapel; in the majority the Anglican parish church will be the only place of worship in the community. Someone ought to advise any Christian moving into the country to check out the local church before buying the house. It is amazing how many Christians do not.

For the leader there is no escape from the responsibility of leadership. This is not an argument for domineering or insensitive leadership. In the church, leadership is a form of service, not a form of tyranny (Mark 10:42–45). But leadership is essential, and it is a gift from God. 'That the leaders took the lead in Israel, that the people offered themselves willingly, bless the

Lord' (Judg 5:2 RSV). A church without firm leadership is in fact being led by one or more of its members. When leaders shrink from the responsibility, and perhaps the odium, of leadership the church is exposed to factional fighting, rivalry and division. The leader must listen to God and to other people who may also hear from God, but there will come a time when he must make up his mind and stick to it.

The canon law of the Church of England says of the music in church:

> Where there is an organist or choirmaster the minister shall pay due heed to his advice and assistance in the choosing of chants, hymns, anthems, and other settings and in the ordering of the music of the church; but at all times the final responsibility and decision in these matters rests with the minister.' (Canon B.20:2)

I had listened to the organist. I had listened to the choir and the music group, and I had listened to the congregation. In the end I had to make the decision: we would sing the old hymns, and we would sing the new songs too. Those who did not like that would have to put up with it or leave.

President Truman knew that the buck had to stop somewhere. It is the job of the church leader to be the place where it stops in the church.

—

TWENTY NINE

I WILL BRING THEM IN

A TRAVELLER IN the west of Ireland stopped to ask the way. 'Can you tell me the way to Ballybunion?' he said. 'Well, it's like this,' the Irishman replied. 'If I was goin' to Ballybunion I would not be starten from here.'

A church leader faced with the task of leading an old, established church into renewal must often share the same sentiments. There is something very attractive about the role of the house church leader or the pioneer church-planter who is able to start from scratch with a clean sheet—no buildings, no traditions, no expectations except his own, no congregation. It is like the builder moving onto a green field site, virgin land waiting to be developed.

The leader of an established church, on the other hand, inherits a vast amount of clutter, some of which may prove useful and useable, some of which is just plain clutter: buildings which may be anything from thirty to a thousand years old, designed for worship and meeting no doubt, but probably for worship and meetings of a very different style from that of today; traditions of how things have always been done, some of which have been set into legal prescriptions about how things must be done; expectations of the leader's role which have little to do with a New Testament understanding of the body of Christ; and a congregation, large or small, who both as individuals and as a corporate body already have a history of their own. The leader has to cope with all of these as he seeks to lead the church into spiritual renewal.

But it is, I believe, a valid vocation, especially in a country which has long been a part of Christendom and already has a long Christian history. There is a time and a place (even today) for the building of Solomon, for the erection of the first temple. But there is also a time and a place for the building of Nehemiah, the rebuilding of the city of God amid the ruins. There will be times when, like Nehemiah's labourers, we feel driven to complain, 'There is so much rubble that we cannot rebuild the wall' (Neh 4:10), but, like them, we will just have to persevere, moving the left-overs of previous walls, reusing some bits and discarding others, and building again that city which is the joy of the whole earth.

The principal problem faced by the church leader seeking to lead an historic church into renewal is that of tradition or, since tradition is not monolithic but varies from denomination to denomination and from place to place, traditions. In fact it is not even traditions in themselves that constitute the obstacle, but traditionalism. By this I mean that state of affairs where the traditions have become the object of worship rather than the living God. It is a state of idolatry, but all the more insidious because the idols are dressed up in Christian apparel and have Christian names.

It is the same problem which crucified the Lord. This was the heart of Jesus' complaint against the

Pharisees and the teachers of the Jews (the traditional-
ist Church). 'You have let go of the commands of God
and are holding on to the traditions of men' (Mark 7:8).
The church leader who embarks upon this course must
be prepared for opposition from those who teach as
doctrines the precepts of men. We also have to be
prepared to meet such opposition in the same spirit in
which Jesus met it, not returning evil with evil or insult
with insult but overcoming evil with good.

Traditionalism is a false god because it leads people
away from that radical trust and obedience which is
what the Bible means by faith. The attraction of it is the
security which it seems to offer. Faith is always elusive
and risky; traditionalism is safe and reassuring. The
father of all those who have faith is Abraham, who left
everything that was safe and reassuring in a risky
adventure of obedience to the word of God. Eventually
the physical descendants of Abraham came to put their
trust in circumcision, which was safe and reassuring,
and forgot that Abraham was justified by faith. In the
same way we Christians can come to worship our traditions, and fail to respond both to the word of God and
to the activity of God before our very eyes.

The saddest part of leading an old church into
renewal is finding fellow church members, who otherwise seem to be leading faithful and even exemplary
lives, unable or unwilling to see what God is doing
today. I regret to say that this is particularly true of my
fellow clergy. The Church of England has its own in-
house way of dealing with people who think they have
something to say to it. They are labelled. After that they
can be safely ignored. People like me are labelled 'charismatics', and fellow church members thereafter feel
themselves justified in looking the other way when we

come by. One wants to weep, as Jesus wept, because they do not recognise the time of God's visitation.

Within the local church traditionalism obstructs the work of renewal. It will not have escaped the reader's attention that of the two churches about which I have written renewal has proceeded much faster at St. Nicholas' than at St. George's. There were very few traditionalists at St. Nicholas', and the ones that were there were not in any of the positions of authority or power within the church. The church had reached a very low point in the early 1960s, but a succession of evangelical clergy had lifted it out of that spiritual death and laid a firm foundation of personal faith and respect for the Scriptures. At St. George's the low point spiritually had been reached in the late 1970s and my predecessor had been battling with the legacy of that. But I inherited a congregation where traditionalism was still much stronger and more firmly entrenched. So the progress of spiritual renewal there has been much slower and harder. But it has progressed.

Among churches elsewhere there will certainly be those like St. Nicholas', ready to take the fast track to renewal, but there will certainly be others like St. George's, which have to take the slow track.

It is important to realise that having identified the problem as one of traditions it is nevertheless not solved in those terms—not solved simply by substituting a new set of traditions for the old. This is a real temptation and a real danger. It is no good simply substituting modern songs for Victorian hymns or noise and informality for quiet solemnity. The problem of traditionalism arises when the attention of people and their worship is focused on the church and its services and not on God himself. It is always discernible in people's conversation: do they talk about the church or about Jesus? Do they talk about the services or about the Lord? The only solution to the problem of traditionalism is to move people's attention and worship to where it rightly belongs—to God himself, his word and his activity.

There was another traveller in the west of Ireland. This one was travelling by train. As the journey progressed the train went slower and slower. Eventually it slowed to walking pace, and then went slower still. At this point the impatient traveller got out and walked up alongside the crawling train until he reached the engine. 'Can't you go any faster than this?' he scolded the driver. 'Of course I can,' the engine-driver replied, 'but I've got to stay with the train.'

A church leader faced with the task of leading an established church into renewal must often share those sentiments too. Again the role of the house church leader or the pioneer church-planter can seem very attractive. But it is part of the calling in this particular work to stay with the train, however slowly it may seem to be moving. This is not an act of cowardice but an act of faith.

When the people of Israel were journeying through the desert after the Exodus from Egypt, they came very soon to a place called Kadesh near the southern border of Canaan. From there they sent spies up into the Promised Land with a view to going in and taking possession of it straightaway. But the spies brought back such adverse tales of the strength of their enemies that the people refused to go on. At this point God gave to Moses (the engine-driver) the opportunity to go on alone. But Moses said that it would be better, not for him, but for the name of God, if he stayed with the train. Without him the people would certainly turn back to Egypt and perish, and then the nations would say, 'The Lord was not able to bring these people into the land he promised them' (Num 14:16). So God and Moses persevered, even with those faithless and perverse people. They had to wander in the wilderness until all those who had refused to enter the Promised Land had died. They had to wait until the people had learned the lesson that there was only one way for them to go, God's way.

Moses is a wonderful model for the church leader leading an old church into renewal. The people will come quite soon to a Kadesh, where they can say yes or no to renewal. From there, there is a quick way into the Promised Land if the people say yes. This, perhaps unusually, is what the people of St. Nicholas' said. But if the corporate answer, if the weight of opinion at this stage is refusal, the leader has only two alternatives. He can leave the people, abandon them to the death they have chosen, and go on alone—perhaps by joining the house church movement—claiming the promise of God 'I will make you into a nation greater and stronger than they' (Num 14:12). Or more like Moses, he can choose to stay with the people for as long as it takes. This is the slow track to renewal. It takes much patience and perseverance. It is necessary to wait while those who have said no leave or change or die, and while God raises up a new generation of Christians within the church who are saying yes to renewal. Pray that it does not take forty years, as it did for Moses. My own experience is that we tend to overestimate how much can change in a year and underestimate how much can change in five years.

The ministry of Moses, of the church leader, is to keep faith in the promises and purposes of God. Before starting out on this adventure of leading a church into renewal, the leader needs to settle within himself that this is not just a whim or fancy of his own, but the very will and purpose of God himself. He can then persevere through all the disappointments and setbacks in the knowledge that God will bring his people to their destination in the end. That is the essential faith: not that I can do it, but that God will do it.

The leader must keep hold of the vision of the land of promise which lies ahead. The patterns of life in that land may not be clearly defined and may not emerge before the people get there, but the leader must keep faith in the existence of that land and God's commitment to bringing his people in.

THIRTY

TEACHING THEM TO OBEY

T HE VISION IS plain. The details may vary from place to place and from denomination to denomination, but the vision must be that of a church renewed in its first love and zeal: as it was at the beginning, a fellowship witnessing boldly to Jesus, doing signs and wonders in his name, filled with the joy of the Lord, feeding daily on the word of God, loving one another with an awesome love, giving and sharing their money and possessions, always hungry for prayer and worship.

But how do we get from where we are to where we want to be? For it is equally plain that that is not where most of the older, longer-established churches are. For most of the church members in those churches, going to church is more a duty than a joy, and a service that lasts more than an hour is regarded as something of an imposition. Coffee mornings are more frequent than prayer meetings. Funds are raised by all manner of degrading means: God is given jumble. Churchgoers like to keep a good distance from one another, and even to ignore one another in the name of devotion. People are ignorant of the Bible, and are more familiar with the women's magazines than the word of God. Joy is absent in their worship and in their lives. God never does miracles because he is never asked; indeed, if it happened, a miracle would probably be ignored or explained away. People are too embarrassed to mention Jesus, regarding their religion as a private matter. The bolder souls will talk about the church, but no-one mentions Jesus. How do we get from where we are, to where we want to be?

I hope it is clear that what has happened at St. Nicholas' and St. George's is not the result of any plans of mine. I did not arrive with plans, and I have not made plans.

Our generation is in love with planning. There may recently have been some disenchantment with State planning but corporate planning is still the gospel for industry and commerce, and many a church leader, looking for a role model in business management, has sought to apply the techniques of corporate planning to the local church. I know churches under the leadership of men I respect where everything is planned six months in advance. As for the services, not only is the preacher planned, but the subject about which he will preach is planned too. In one parish where I served as a curate, the Winter Programme was published each year in September, with details of all the church meetings and the activities of all its organizations planned through to the following Easter. In the past I have often devised plans for myself, for visiting those on the church membership roll, for visiting whole areas from door to door; I have made lists of baptisms and funerals to be followed up, and lists of the housebound and elderly to be visited at regular intervals. So the days and the months have filled up with my plans.

There are schools of thought in the church today that are applying corporate planning methods to mission. The Decade of Evangelism seems to be encouraging this tendency. We are urged to collect data, set goals for growth, motivate the membership, train, evaluate, plan, plan, plan. First it was planning for growth in the local church, now it is planning for the growth of more churches. Perhaps all this is inevitable: not only is it the way of the world in which we live, but it reflects our own recent history of evangelism. Evangelism for the last forty years has been virtually synonymous with Billy Graham, and if not with him personally then with the sort of highly organized crusades for which his name stands. Now the methods may be more varied (I was sent a list of eighty ideas for parish evangelism recently) but the urge to plan it all still persists. It is as if we fear that if we do not plan it nothing will happen.

I believe that the opposite is more nearly the case. Of course there is the need for administration—any sort of working together as a body requires some organization and administration, and the bigger the church the more organization and administration will undoubtedly be required. But that is not the same as planning. Too much planning crowds God out. It is not up to us to plan what God is going to do or how he is going to do it. God undoubtedly has plans; he has had the whole thing planned since before the foundation of the world (Eph 1:3–10). It is also true that he discloses something of his plans beforehand to his servants the prophets (Amos 3:7). But if he does so it is not so that we can take over and fix things up for him; it is simply so that he gets the glory when it comes to pass.

The fact is that God's thoughts are not our thoughts (Is 55:8), and God's plans are not our plans. God is supremely unpredictable and he does not fit into our programmes for him. No-one has ever succeeded in programming God. My own experience is that God often does the most exciting things while I am looking the other way, and his most important acts are often the ones I least expect. How do you make plans for a God of surprises? The sad thing is that the more we try to do so, the less room we leave for God.

My 'strategy' for St. Nicholas' and St. George's was simply to let God have his way among us. I knew how ineffectual my own efforts had been. By the time I came to these two churches I was willing to let God have a go. My ministry here has been an ongoing experiment in seeing what God can do. My job here has been to see what God is doing and bless it. It means a hands-off approach, rather than hands-on. It means letting other people hear from God, as much as me, and respecting what they then say and do. It means letting people make mistakes (including myself). It means letting God do unexpected, and sometimes strange, things. It means being more fearful of interfering with what God is doing, than of things getting out of hand. It means trusting God to know what he is doing, and trusting God to be in control. For a clergyman or pastor that means a colossal letting go.

There is a need for oversight and there is a need for order, but it needs to be God's order, which is not always as neat and tidy as ours. There is a need for authority, and everyone, including the leader himself, needs to know where that authority lies. In fact the ministry of exercising authority comes into a sharper focus in a Spirit-filled church. As with children and adolescents in the home, people in a church that is open to the Spirit need the security of knowing that someone is in authority. There are other spirits around; there can be manifestations which are disorderly or disturbing. People can only relax and enjoy the freedom of the Spirit in the assurance that things are not going to be allowed to go spiritually wrong. But this authority is essentially the authority that Jesus gives over the power of the enemy; it is not an authority to dominate the lives of others and it is certainly not authority at all over what the Sovereign Lord chooses to do.

There are, however, two vital functions for the church leader to fulfil if a church is to move from death to life: one is to minister the word, and the other to minister the Spirit to the people. What the Lord said to the prophet Ezekiel was 'Speak to these bones', and the operative word is 'speak'. There is no renewal in the church without a renewal of the ministry of the word. This means primarily, though by no means exclusively, the ministry of preaching. I have actually heard it said that the day of the sermon as a means of communication is over. No doubt that is true of some sermons. But I continue to be astonished at the power of anointed preaching. The miracle is that God uses our words as we expound his word to bring about life-giving change in the hearers.

The preacher himself needs to sit under and live under the word of God in Scripture. He must preach the good news, the full gospel of healing and salvation, of deliverance and victory in the name of Jesus. And he must preach for a response, not once but continuously, expecting God to effect the changes in people's lives which Jesus came to make possible. It is a costly and daunting ministry, for the gospel will not be universally welcome. It never was. We servants cannot expect to be received any better than our master.

As I have proved, it is a ministry that involves many a spiritual battle, which is not so much a matter of sitting in prayer meetings and saying, 'We come against the spirit of...', nor is it a matter of marching round the village saying, 'We claim this ground for the Lord.' It is principally a matter of facing down the enemy in concrete situations, doing what has to be done, saying what has to be said. It is a matter of overcoming the fear of man, not least the fear of bishops and other authority figures, the fear of elders or deacons or church councils, the fear of people leaving, the fear of everything going wrong.

But if these fears are quenched with the shield of faith, it is a ministry of great peace. For if it is truly God's work and not our own, then we can safely leave it to him. The problems that arise are not our problems but his. It is not my reputation that is at stake, but his. It is not my church anyway, but his. So I sleep soundly at night, whatever the ructions going on in the churches and the parishes, trusting him to sort it out to his glory and praise.

But even the ministry of the word is not sufficient by itself. As Ezekiel prophesied to the dead bones, the bones came together; tendons, flesh and skin appeared to cover them, but still there was no breath in them. Then God spoke to the prophet a second time and said, 'Speak to the breath'. The church leader must also preach and minister the baptism of the Holy Spirit.

I know there are Christians, especially those who are theologically educated, who stumble at this. There are many who dogmatically hold that we received all that there is of the Holy Spirit when we were converted, or when we were baptised in water, or perhaps when we were confirmed. I also know that none of these things is true. Being baptised in the Holy Spirit is essentially a separate event from being born again; it is not identical with either of the outward and visible signs of baptism in water or confirmation. It sometimes happens that baptism in the Spirit occurs in close proximity to one or other of these events, but it is not to be confused with any of them.

I have seen ample evidence of this at first hand in the lives of many people, some of whose stories I have told in this book. When people who are born again spiritually, baptised or confirmed as they may be, seek the baptism of the Holy Spirit their lives are changed again. The baptism of the Spirit is not to be confused with some other experience of spiritual refreshment or indeed with any other supernatural experience. It is the Pentecostal outpouring which every believer needs and has a right and a duty to receive, but which, for some reason, many older churchgoers resist. But it is the Holy Spirit who is the Lord and giver of life, and both Christians and churches will remain dead bones until they are filled with the Holy Spirit.

Some people, especially the theologically sophisticated, want to hold back until they understand all this. I was one of those for ten long years. But that is not the way God works. Adam and Eve did not understand the reason for the forbidden fruit, and because they did not understand they disobeyed: that is sin. Abraham did not understand the reason for leaving Ur of the Chaldeans, but he obeyed all the same: that is blessing. Augustine said, 'I believe in order to understand'; not, 'I understand in order to believe.' Obedience comes first; understanding comes after.

So, finally, anyone who would seek to speak to the dry bones of God's people and lead an old church or a new church into life must first seek the baptism of the Holy Spirit for himself. Jesus said, '...stay in the city until you have been clothed with power from on high' (Luke 24:49). In other words, stay at home until you have received the baptism of the Holy Spirit. But unlike the first disciples I do not believe that we have to wait, only ask: 'Dear Father, I ask you to baptise me with the Holy Spirit, as you did the first disciples on the day of Pentecost, in your Son Jesus' name.' Then go out and teach others the same. God will take it from there.

There is no renewal of the church without the renewal of individuals in the Holy Spirit. There are no short cuts. Introducing guitars, teaching people new songs, even getting people to perform actions while they sing, is not spiritual renewal. The renewal of the baptism of the Holy Spirit has to take place in one believer after another: every individual Christian has to seek and find this for themselves. But yet the renewal of a church is more than just the renewal of individual Christians. It is possible to have a church leader baptised in the Spirit and many of the congregation baptised in the Spirit too, and yet nothing in the church as a whole seems to change. The church is in the grip of ancient principalities and powers. They have to be faced and faced down. It is hard and painful, no sort of easy option. But the victory is the Lord's.

—

EPILOGUE

A s I FINISH this book, I know what the Evangelist John meant when he finished his: 'Jesus did many other things as well. If every one of them were written down, I suppose that even the whole world would not have room for the books that would be written' (John 21:25). Jesus has done so many other things in our two churches in these few years that I have not the room to include. I hope that the people whose stories I have not been able to tell will understand why I have had to leave them out.

This has been the story of the stumbling and fumbling efforts of very ordinary people in two very ordinary churches to follow Jesus at the end of the twentieth century. But we have proved again in our own experience that Jesus is alive and can still do the things which he did on earth twenty centuries ago. We have proved in our own experience that the same power is available to the church today as was available at the beginning, the power of the Holy Spirit. It was a power which in an incredibly short time turned the world upside down. The world desperately needs to be turned upside down again today by the same power. The church's only reason for existence is to be the vessel and the channel for that power.

Monarch Publications

Books of Substance

All Monarch books can be purchased from your local
Christian or general bookshop. In case of difficulty they may
be ordered from the publisher:

> Monarch Publications
> Broadway House
> The Broadway
> Crowborough
> East Sussex
> TN6 1HQ

Please enclose a cheque payable to Monarch Publications for
the cover price plus: 60p for the first book ordered plus 40p
per copy for each additional book, to a maximum charge of
£3.00 to cover postage and packing (UK and Republic of
Ireland only).

Overseas customers please order from:

Christian Marketing PTY Ltd
PO Box 154
North Geelong
Victoria 3215
Australia

Kingsway USA Inc
4717 Hunter's Crossing Drive
Old Hickory
TN 37138
USA

Omega Distributors Ltd
69 Great South Road
Remuera
Auckland
New Zealand

Christian Marketing Canada
Box 7000
Niagara-on-the-Lake
Ontario LOS 1JO
Canada

Struik Christian Books
80 McKenzie Street Gardens
Cape Town 8001
South Africa

I Will Pour Out My Spirit

by R. E. Davies

A comprehensive analysis of revivals past and present.

Many writers have tackled the theme of revival, but few have cast their nets so widely or so systematically. Dr Ron Davies looks at revivals in Scripture and throughout history, and also discerns key theological issues.

His topics include:

- Theological and biblical definitions
- The teaching of Jonathan Edwards, the classic theologian of revival
- A survey of major revivals of past and present
- Excesses and other problems accompanying revival
- Is it possible for Christians to 'produce a revival' by prayer?
- Can Christians by their actions bring revival to a premature end?
- What connection is there between revivals and the Second Coming?

'An excellent study. It fills a significant gap in the literature on revival.' — *James Bradley, Professor of Church History, Fuller Theological Semonary*

ISBN 1 85424 160 5   288pp, £9.99

Monarch
Publications

The Gospel Conspiracy

by Michael Marshall

Renewal is both essential—and costly. Without renewal the Church retreats into man-made formalism. Renewal occurs as we confront God revealed in Jesus.

'Renewal is costly,' states Michael Marshall, 'because it leads to the reformation of society. Magellan discovered the world was round by sailing closer to the edge than anyone else before him! That is precisely where and how the Church needs to sail today—closer to the edges, where it can prove the power and truth of its gospel, challenging the prejudices and blindnesses of society, a society that is weary and largely spent.'

Bishop Michael Marshall has been a university chaplain and a vicar in London before becoming Bishop of Woolwich in 1975. In 1984 he founded the Anglican Institute in St Louis, Missouri, and in 1992 returned to the UK to head, with Michael Green, the Springboard Initiative set up by Archbishop George Carey.

'Michael Marshall's writing is both gospelly and unchurchy; indeed it amounts to a gale of fresh air rushing through old stuffinesses, throwing back shutters, and bringing in sheer health. It is God-centred, Christ-centred, self-abandoning. It is apologetic with a warm human face; it is good news which is truly divine.'
Bishop Colin Buchanan, *Church Times*

ISBN 1 85424 187 7   192pp, £6.99

Monarch
Publications

The Bondage Breaker

by Neil T. Anderson

Overcoming negative thoughts, irrational feelings and
habitual sins.

You find yourself locked in habits you can't break. You're a
Christian and this sort of thing doesn't happen to
Christians—or so you've been told.

You can break free! The Bible warns repeatedly that all
Christians will struggle against Satan. While the conflict is
real, so are the answers. This solidly biblical book reminds
us that our struggle involves more than sinful desires and
psychological disorders. Dr Anderson guides us in God's
practical means and provisions for victory.

'Such spiritual common sense... I am very impressed.
Down to earth and practical.'—Gerald Coates

'*The Bondage Breaker* gives balance. This book teaches the
Christian how to be personally responsible for overcoming
the powers of opposition in his or her life. I thoroughly
recommend it.'—Colin Urquhart

ISBN 1 85424 184 2   256pp. £3.99

Monarch
Publications

Victory Over the Darkness

by Neil T. Anderson

Realising the power of your identity in Christ.

'Being in Christ, and all that it means to Christian identity and freedom, is the overwhelming theme of the New Testament...if you see yourself as a child of God who is spiritually alive in Christ, you'll begin to live in victory and freedom.'

Every day millions of Christians live below par—emotionally, physically, spiritually. Because they do not grasp the central fact of their identity in Christ, they miss out on the freedom and maturity they should enjoy. This life-transforming book is for everyone who longs for spiritual growth.

'I cannot recommend this book highly enough... *Victory Over the Darkness* points the way to true liberty and victory in Jesus.'—Colin Urquhart.

ISBN 1 85424 183 4   256pp, £3.99

Monarch
Publications

Warfare Prayer

by C. Peter Wagner

Since 1987 Dr Peter Wagner has been researching prayer.
This is the first of a series of books resulting from that
research, and deals with strategic-level spiritual warfare.

'Certain subjects are handled in some depth in this book
which have so far not found their way into print,' he
explains. 'I have included more biblical material here than I
have found in any other book, partly because many are
questioning whether there is biblical warrant for strategic-
level spiritual warfare at all.

'The concepts of spiritual territoriality and the naming of
powers have received considerable attention here. Holiness
is frequently mentioned in other books, bur rarely is it
analyzed in the depth I believe is required for effective
warfare prayer.

'This may sound like a scholarly treatise. I hope it has
scholarly integrity, but each chapter is full of lively
stories... My prayer is that those who are hearing what the
Spirit is saying will find this book an instrument in God's
hands to draw them closer to Himself and to open them in
a new way to powerful warfare prayer.'

ISBN 1 85424 173 7   208pp, £7.99

Monarch
Publications